If Memory Could Speak

If Memory Could Speak

Sukadev Nanda

BLACK EAGLE BOOKS
Dublin, USA | BBSR, India

Black Eagle Books
USA address:
7464 Wisdom Lane
Dublin, OH 43016

India address:
E/312, Trident Galaxy, Kalinga Nagar,
Bhubaneswar-751003, Odisha, India

E-mail: info@blackeaglebooks.org
Website: www.blackeaglebooks.org

First International Edition Published by
Black Eagle Books, 2022

IF MEMORY COULD SPEAK
by **Sukadev Nanda**

Original Copyright © Sukadev Nanda

All rights reserved. No part of this publication may be reproduced, stored in a retrieval system, or transmitted, in any form or by any means, electronic, mechanical, photocopying, recording or otherwise without the prior permission of the publisher.

Cover & Interior Design: Ezy's Publication

ISBN- 978-1-64560-315-3 (Paperback)
Library of Congress Control Number: 9781645603153

Printed in the United States of America

Dedicated
to the loving memory of my
Bā

ACKNOWLEDGEMENT

For preparation of this small book giving some details of me, my background, friends and pears, associated institution, my village and dimensions of its sweetness, besides my achievements and failures, I have been indebted to several person. They include the young boys who did the field work for me, my cousin Shyam Sundar Dash (Ura Bhaina) who coordinated the efforts at his level in the village and gave me details about the families which have risen quite high and those which have faced a decline. I am also thankful to Prof. B M Otta, retired Professor of Fakir Mohan University for the help he has extended at each stage of the work. He also has helped me in correcting the typed script and facilitating publication of this small book. I am thankful to Satyajit (Tutu), Biswajit (Mantu) and Niranjan for the way they helped in gathering information and photographs of the village. I express my grateful thanks to my friend Prof. Dinesh Prasad Pattnaik and Haraprasad Das for their useful comments before publication of this book.

    I also thank my three sons in law (Biswamohan, Amulya ratna and Sunil), the three daughters (Arati, Shashwati and Shrabanti). My thanks are also due to my grandson Anewesh and granddaughter Ashavaree for the assistance and encouragement they have provided to me. It is needless to thank my wife Renu though she has always been with me, in all situations.

PREFACE

Right from the childhood, I was intensely committed to my village, I came out it in 1961 to pursue higher education in Ravenshaw College and, Utkal University. I visited the village as and when opportunity was available. I worked for a short while in the P.G.Dept. of Utkal University in 1967 and later joined the Berhampur University in November, 1968. Till I left this University for Sambalpur University in Jan, 1978, my visit to the village and association with my friends in the village continued at regular intervals. My mother expired in 1982 (Sept.) and my adoptive father whom I loved the most also expired in 1989. My father stayed most of the time at Bhubaneswar and therefore, I did not feel much inclined to visit the village hereafter though I came there, moved about, had darshan of Goddess Sarla and went back. Even without coming to the village, I always remembered it, its beautiful sites, places of importance, the Mahadev temple, the Padma Pokhari etc. The Kartik Purnima always reminded me of Mahadev temple, Fakir Muduli and Gaja Prasad. Pana Sankranti reminded me of the way we in childhood, distributed curd-water-Mahaprasad to the pilgrims who came to visit Goddess Sarala. The famous Kakara of Sarala temple on Mahastami almost took me for some time to Kanakpur on this occasion. I always speak to my children about the beautiful flavour of chudaghasa prasad of Goddes Sarala.

Probably ma Sarala did not approve my plan to spend my old age in the village. I accept it with all pleasure.

Even since I came across studies made by different scholars on villages, I cherished a desire to do some work on my own village and its adjoining ones and examine the extent to which there have been changes and whether these changes have been in the desired directions. Since I myself conducted some work on villages elsewhere, I planned to do this work after my retirement. On my retirement in April, 2003, I started planning for it in preparing a project for presentation to the UGC for funding. Before I could make much headway in the matter, I was given the responsibility of building a new university (F. M. University). My attention was totally shifted to the new business. I devoted my whole time and energy to the new-born university. In March, 2008, I retired for this position but visiting my son at London and thereafter, different national level academic assignments, UGC Committee membership, assignments of National Assessment and Accreditation Council (NAAC) kept me preoccupied. However, I prepared a questionnaire and planned to have the field work done by the Research Scholars of an old friend and complete the Work. Then came the rude shock- my only son left me forever and then a former Professor of F.M. University, who lost his job during my Vice-Chancellorship filed a defamation and compensation case for Rs.5 lakhs and his wife (for her husband's loss of job caused defame) filed a case for compensation of Rupees fifty lakhs. Someone, (Probably this gentleman) made petitions to all possible investigating agencies against alleged corruption committed by me. I was in the ocean of grief. Hereafter for three years, I had frequent health failures and hospitalization. The work remained at that stage, no field work was possible.

It was at this stage that I had pressures from some friends and well-wishers to write a memoir and give an account of developments made in Fakir Mohan University as also the help and cooperation given by several people and institutions. They said that writing a memoir is not self-propaganda. It was necessary from the point of view of the society. Having lived a fairly long life and having worked in different capacities in different work places, one has the duty to provide a fact-based record of things for assessment. The posterity may receive positive benefit or even learn how to avoid pitfalls into which they might otherwise fall. Such writings are narrations of experiences of success and the manner of achieving them as also the obstacles which one had to face successfully. Some romanticize their childhood and family and, in course of doing so, they, knowingly or unknowingly, deviate from the path of truth. Basic tenet of memoir writing is truth which I have adhered to. It is a golden principle not to hurt anybody in a memoir. I have deliberately refrained from making any reference to such people who in my opinion, did something undesirable. I have forgotten them and their acts which were uncalled for and undesirable.

This work has been presented in five chapters. Chapter-I (The place I come from) gives a brief account of the village I come from, its beautiful features, the caste structure in the village, inter caste relationship, land ownership etc. A brief attempt has been made here to throw some light on the state of the village and its level of development. In discussing an ordinary oil seller and his method of measurement, an attempt has been made to throw lightv on nthe socioeconomic position of the village and its people. It includes the picture of the rural elite who helped resolution of conflicts. The chapter-II (Me, my friends and family) is devoted to description of my parents, family, relations etc. This is a short one. Chapter-III is on my professional career. I have worked in Utkal, Berhampur, Sambalpur and Fakir Mohan Universities. Whereas I had to devote myself to teaching and research in the first three Universities, I had to work as an educational administrator in F. M. University. Extracurricular work I had to do in one place was different in another. I had a network of friendship in all these places. Having worked in new Universities, (Berhampur and Sambalpur), I had the first-hand information about their problems and about how the successful Vice-Chancellors played their roles. These probably helped me at Balasore. The two chapters (IV and V) relate to my days and activities in Fakir Mohan University. The chapter IV (F. M. University: Efforts for recognition) gives details about the way a university could be established at Balasore. It was at the nascent stage and I had to bring it to a productive institution, various things were to be done, cooperation and help from several persons had to be sought and achieved. The university had to fulfil the conditions necessary for accordance of UGC recognition u/s 12(B) of the UGC Act, 1956. The university had to work like a university and function as such before the UGC Committee visited for grant of recognition.

The Chapter-V (Post recognition developments) gives information about how the university prepared development projects for financing by the UGC and other funding agencies. And how the funds so received were fruitfully utilized in time. Also, in this chapter, I have described how the new campus was built and how the university had to fight evil forces who created various types of difficulties. This chapter also includes my post retirement days.

(Sukadev Nanda)

If Memory Could Speak
INDEX

Chapter-I

The Place I Come From	1
Physical Feature	1
Caste Structure in the village	7
The Scheduled Castes in the village	13
Land and Agriculture	16
The agricultural Workers	18
Adia Teli, the Oil man	19
Village Life	22
Some bases of rural conflict	29
Unproductive Indebtedness	32
Bhadra lok, Bhal lok and Tout	35
Cultural Activities in the Village	36
Educational Facilities	38
Health Care in the Village	43
Some Notable Village Elders	45
The new face of the village	48
Maa Sarala Thakurani	52
The Venerable Sanyasis of Karamala	57
Fairs and Festivities in the Village	62

Chapter-II

Me, My Family and Friends	67
Bhaina & Nuabou	70
Ba's Family	71
Bā adopted me	72
An unintended Shock	73
My Marriage	74

My In Law's Family	75
My Children	78
The House at Niladri Vihar	82
Suman's Marriage	87
Bratopanayan of Anwesh	91
I Visited London	92
Friends, Peers, Happiness and Tears	94
A Blow from the Unknown	97
Met a Spiritual leader	100
My Young Friends	102

Chapter-III

My Professional Career	104
Berhampur University	104
Some Memorable Interactions	109
Sambalpur University	117
My House was like a Hostel: My wife its Warden	127

Chapter-IV

Fakir Mohan University: Efforts for Recognition	129
The Balasore Educational Foundation	129
Balasore-Baripada Divide: Creation of North Odisha University	130
Birth of FM University	132
Fakir Mohan University in Sept, 2003.	132
The Infrastructure of the University	133
The F.M. University Office and Officers	134
Recognition under Section 12(B): The Challenges to be Met	137
Kind Intervention of the Chancellor (Mr. M. M. Rajendran)	140
Selection of Faculties	141
Developments in the Campus	143
Finding Space for the Five Teaching Departments	146
The Library	147
Electricity Supply	150
Healthcare Centre	151
Students Health Insurance	152
Students Assessment of Teachers	152
Communication Skill Development	153

Campus free from Students unrest	153
Cafeteria approach to Courses	155
Memorial Lectures	155
Election to the Senate, Syndicate and Academic Council (July, 2004)	155
University Journals	156
Fakir Mohan National Award in Prose Literature	156
Seminars in the Departments	158
Visiting Professorship	158
Organisation of Refresher Courses	158
Augmentation of Resources	159
Joined the Brihaspati Project	159
Special Care of Accounts- Appointment of a Retired Audit Officer	160
Planned for a Department of Ballistics	160
Visit of the UGC Committee	162
The Celebrations	164

Chapter-V

Post Recognition Developments	165
The Post-recognition Problems	165
Purchase of Books	167
The Special Experience	167
The X Plan allocation utilization and after	168
Preparation of the development proposal for the XI Plan	170
New Departments	170
Distance Education	170
Distance Education branches in University's Development	172
A Printing Unit in the University	173
Undisturbed Electricity Supply	174
Updating disposal of pending degrees and diploma	174
The New Campus: Its initial Challenges	175
The Problems taken to Raj Bhawan	178
The Last Kick	180
Agency for construction work	180
Appointed Engineering Expert Committee	183
Ideas to open new Postgraduate Courses	184
The University- PXE Dialogue	186

Dr. Seelva Murthy delivered Kantakabi Lecture	187
Solicited kind intervention of Dr. Kalam	188
The proposal for Applied Physics and Ballistics with the Government	189
The Aftermath of the decision	193
I failed to have the Department of Languages.	195
The Convocation of the University	195
My father expired	197
The Third Convocation	199
The fourth Convocation: New Campus Inauguration	200
Campus Sanctification	201
Preparation for NAAC Accreditation	202
Efforts to acquire more land	203
Publication of a Monograph of Fakir Mohan	203
Fakir Mohan Archives	204
Chancellors of the University I worked Under	205
Retirement from Fakir Mohan University	209
Balasore and me, after retirement	210
A Vigilance enquiry against me	212
My appointment as a Member of the General Council of NAAC	215
Academic activities after retirement	215
An unforgettable experience	218
Court Cases that followed	220
Friends who helped me at Balasore	221
Niladri Vihar to Durga Madhav Nagar: Shift of Place of Stay	228

Chapter-I

The Place I Come From

Physical Feature

My village, Govindpur, is about five kilometers away from Rathipur on the Cuttack-Paradeep Highway. There is a pucca road connecting Rathipur to my village. The village begins at Taradei Pitha, then comes the Govindpur school complex. It was just a Lower Primary school during our times, now it has developed into a complex of Lower Primary, Upper Primary and High School. The High School building is on a high land close to Padma Pokhari with the Primary School to its west. Between them runs the road that leads to the village. Earlier, there was an open space of about two acres between the school and the village. Now this place has been fruitfully utilized for Government offices and a market complex. Hereafter, begin the rows of houses. During my childhood, the village began with the house of my father Bhagabat Nanda. Now, many new houses have come up before that. The village is quite big, about 1.5 km in length from North to South. There is a common passage of about 15 feet wide from the Padma Pokhari to the southern end of the village. It is called the Dānda. Two parallel rows of dwelling houses are constructed on both sides of the Danda. Most people being farmers, tied their cows, bullocks and calves in front of their houses, making the Danda too congested for free movement.

The Dānda in those days was very reeking with bad smell of urine and cow dung. It sometimes became muddy and quite slippery. Little carelessness could result in difficulties. These days the Dānda is quite clean. People have developed a good taste and they station their animals elsewhere making the Dānda free for movement of vehicles. On both sides of the Dānda were residential thatched houses. During my childhood, there was only one pucca house (Madan Dash). He ran some business at Calcutta. Now, most houses are pucca. There was branch like extensions from the main Dānda of the village. There extension were lanes (called Gohari). Like the main Dānda, passing between the two rows of residential houses, the Goharis also had their houses on both sides. These lanes provided space for meeting the additional need of houses no doubt but these also had other benefits. The farmers went out to their fields (either in the East or west of the village) with their bullocks and the plough through these Goharis.

The number of such Gohari was six. The first Gohari from the Padma Pokhari side is called Nanda Sahi. It was in this Gohari that my father and Bā had their houses. In this lane lived Brahmins with the surnames "Nanda". These days, people having other surnames and castes are living here. The second Gohari is called Nahaka Gohari because it leads to the tank called Nahak Pokhari. It also touches the Ishaneswar Mandir, the Dhoba Sahi (Washer Men Sahi) and Gauda Sahi (Milk Men Sahi). Functional Castes like Dhoba, Gauda, Chamar etc. as also some Khandayats stayed at the end of the Nahaka Gohari. Beyond these houses, the Gohari leads to some other villages.

There is a big cemented platform in the Dānda wherefrom originates the Nahaka Gohari. It was called Badachaurā. It was on this high platform that the village elders met for deciding on issues affecting and benefiting the village. Also, they sat as a court to settle disputes among villagers. Many people sat here in the evening to while away their time. The Annual Asta Prahari (Nam Yagna) was held near this Bada Chaurā in front of the house of Lokei Rout.

The third Gohari is known as Chautara Gohari. While the Nanda Gohari and the Nahaka Gohari lead to the east from the main Dānda, the Chautara Gohari leads to the west of the main Dānda. This Gohari ends near the canal wherefrom people go either to their agricultural farms or out of the village to the shopping center at Kanakpur, or the Thakurani Market. The canal embankment remained crowded on Thursdays and Sundays as these were the weekly market days.

Earlier, there was no bridge over the canal. We had to wade through the water to cross it. At times, when the water was full, we could not cross the canal. Men, women and animals had their bath in this canal. The fourth Gohari is comparatively smaller one and it is not far from the third. It may be 200 meters or so away from the third Gohari.

The Dash Sahi (Dash Families) starts after Chautara Gohari and ends at the fourth Gohari. This Gohari is the smallest of all the lanes. About six Dhoba families and a few Khandayat families live here. Then comes the fifth Gohari which is between the houses of Pradhan families and Mohanty families. It is a big lane and home to many propertied people here. The last Gohari at the southern end of the village, unlike other Goharis, has only one row of houses. This ultimately leads to the southern part of the canal where the chautara gohari met. The majority in the village constitute the Khandayats (also known as Chasa) followed by the Brahmins whose number is limited to about twenty families.

Accessibility: My Village Govindpur is in Jagatsinghpur District. It was about 5kms away from a Motorable road at Dānda Sahi from where one could travel in a bus to Cuttack and other places. One had to walk down this distance since, in those days, there was no conveyance like a rickshaw or auto rickshaw. Walking down the distance was not a problem, since, as rural folk, we had the habit of walking. It was a problem only because there was no road from our village to Dāndasahi. One had to walk on the hedges in the rice fields where sometimes venomous serpents were encountered abruptly. Therefore, When I came to take admission in the Ravenshaw college in June, 1961, my Bā accompanied me. He carried a stick in his hand and I followed him. Our domestic help carried my luggage while crossing the agricultural field. I put on a lungi and a banian and carried my full pant, shirt and shoes in a small bag. This was because, for most part of the distance, we had to walk in knee-deep water. Sometimes also, the way was extremely muddy and that anything like chappals would be fully spoilt once used on such a path. Conditions started improving in 1970s when Kanakpur was connected by road.

Instead of going to Dāndasahi, one could board the bus at Kanakpur or the Thakurani Hāt. For this, the route from my village to the Thakurani Hat was the embarkment of the canal. It was better than the earlier route, yet, it had also problems. In the rainy season, the embarkment became muddy and the canal contained maximum water. The embarkment was not very wide and if careless, one could slip into the canal water.

These days, such problems no longer exist. The canal embankment is now motorable and in all season, we do not have any problem to reach our village in a car, jeep, bike or even by walk. Number of autorickshaws is so many that one can easily take their help from the village to places outside. Besides, most families have bikes, scooters and four wheelers for the purpose of their movement.

The Dānda of our village and its Goharis are now cemented roads and the village has more than 15 four wheelers, a large number of Motor Cycles, Scooters etc. The present generation may find it difficult to believe the picture of our days.

Not only that, right from the beginning of the Village at Taradei Pith, a pucca road goes to Kinalo via Ishaneswar Mandir, the canal embankment having been made motorable, the village is very well accessible. It is equally so in case of most other nearby villages.

The Padma Pokhari: On the North side of the village, there lies a big tank of rectangular shape, occupying more than an acre of land. This is known as the Padma Pokhari (Lotus tank). In its north lie a branch canal and the village called Sahans. On the western side of Padma Pokhari are the village schools. On the eastern side there is an open space of more than two acres. Between the village and the Padma Pokhari lay a big patch of open and uneven land, which was used earlier as the playground for the children. The space in the west was mainly used as the village Shamsan (cremation ground) as also the space for open defecation by the villagers. It was the dirtiest of all the four sides. Because of the uneven nature of the land, rain water went into the tank from the southern and the western sides. As a result, the water became highly polluted and unfit for any kind of human use.

Padma Pokhari

Padma Pokhari is a misnomer. I have never seen any Lotus in this tank. My elders also said so. May be, long ago, Lotus flowers blossomed in this tank. However, Padma Pokhari looked very beautiful during the rainy season when Lily flowers, in very large number, blossomed in it. During our childhood days, we collected lots of these flowers and used them in decorating our houses. Some of my friends loved to swim is the tank. People made multiple use of the tank; they bathed, cleaned themselves in the tank after open defecation, and the women also washed their dirty clothes. The cattle of the village were also taken into the tank for a bath. In course of time, too much of wild plants grown in the tank polluted the water which became unfit for human use.

This village tank was used by the Brahmins and other touchable caste people. Those belonging to scheduled castes used other tanks in the village. Dhoba, Bauri and Doms, however, had no difficulty in going into the tank and catching fish for the high castes though they were not allowed to bathe. The funeral ground lying in the western side of the tank was earmarked for Brahmins and other high caste people. A small area, near the Othaka tank, close to the Bauri Sahi, was reserved for the Nanda and Dash Sahi

Brahmins. The scheduled castes, treated as untouchables, had their funeral ground at a place away from that of the Brahmins and other high castes. These ideas seem to have disappeared these days.

In earlier days, during summer months of March-April, when the water level of the tank went down, the villagers caught fish and distributed it among themselves. With the emergence of Panchatiraj system, particularly after the Constitutional Amendment giving enormous power to local government institution, the Panchayat has full control over such tanks. This tank has been a big source of revenue for the village Panchayat. However, it is alleged that there is some maneuvering made by some in the management of fishing in Padma Pokhari, resulting in interest groups fighting among themselves for the management of this village tank.

These days, the picture of the Padma Pokhari and its vicinity has significantly changed. Open defecation having been banned by the government, chances of polluting the water has been minimized though not fully eliminated. Padma Pokhari is no more used by one and all for bathing. People have, now, their private arrangement of bath at their own houses. A good number of government offices have come up in the area. With the development of road connectivity in and around the village, there is road leading to the Padma Pokhari. Some small shops have been opened. The Padma Dānda is no longer desolate and fearful.

Caste Structure in the village

Caste refers to hereditary group of people based on traditional pattern of stratification. The Hindus are hierarchically divided into varna, caste and often sub-caste that determined their social position. However, in a village like mine, the castes were functionally related to each other as an organic whole. Each caste has its own organization, primarily to enforce caste discipline over its members. Unlike these days, these caste organizations did not have political affiliations. Inter caste marriages were generally forbidden and punishable particularly among higher castes. Apart from the traditional stratification system, economic inequality cut across caste lines to make the socio-cultural status even more complicated.

My village has a history of caste amity and cooperation. We never knew of caste conflict until we reached the urban centre. In my village, Brahmins occupied the highest position in the caste hierarchy although they constituted less than 10% of the families of the village. Most Brahmins worked as priests in the neighboring and distant villages. Like all other caste groups, some of the Brahmins of my village did not stick to their traditional occupation. They migrated to far off urban areas looking for other occupations. Some of them specialized in cooking and had reputation of being excellent chefs and, thus, had a wide market in marriage seasons. Compared to people of all other castes, Brahmins were more educated and more numerous as government employees. Quite a few of them were school teachers in local villages. Some occupied administrative positions in state and central governments.

The Khandayats were the dominant caste in the village from the point of view of their numerical strength and economic position. Brahmins alone were ritually above them. A ritually lower caste could become dominant by virtue of its economic, political and numerical strength. Their dominance was also demonstrated through their land holding and extent of land transfers. They, however, remained engaged in agricultural operations throughout the year although their mode of agriculture was outdated. My Bhaina (eldest brother) had a role in modernizing agriculture in our village. Fertilizers and pesticides were first introduced by him in our agricultural land and it probably motivated others to emulate.

The Khandayats cultivated paddy and pulses, such as black gram, green gram and, at times ground nut. Currently the variety of crops and the yield speak of the advances made in agriculture by villagers. The surpluses, then produced, were disposed off at the local market but the volume of production having gone high and communication having been opened up, its disposal now, is done in urban centers. Some of the farmers had their bullock-carts which they used in agricultural operations as also a mode of local transport at a cost. In those days, a newly married woman moved in bullock-carts when she came to her parents' place and when she returned therefrom. During my childhood, I remember, Ratani Rout and Fakir Muduli from our village possessing the most sought-after bullock carts in the area. Travel in their carts was comfortable. I accompanied my cousin sister to her in-law's house in a bullock cart.

The other castes in the village included Gauda (Milk Man), Bhandari (Barber), Bania (Jewellers), Gudia (Sweet makers), Keuta (Fish Catchers) and Scheduled Castes like Dhoba (Washer man), Dom (Drum man), Chamar (Brewer), Bauri etc. The Gaudas had cows and they supplied milk and the milk products (such as curd and ghee). Besides, they also carried loads of goods from one house to another. The Barbers shaved the villagers and received their remuneration in form of some paddy on an annual basis. Also, they received some money and clothes from their customers on special occasions like marriage, upanayan or death in families. They worked in the agricultural fields as wage earners too. The Keutas prepared Chuda (crushed and pressed rice) and caught fish from local water bodies and rivers. The Doms, Bauris and Chamars belonged to the untouchable category. The Doms prepared bamboo-baskets and bamboo-made household commodities. They played the drums on ceremonial occasions in the houses of higher caste families. The Bauris worked in agricultural fields and also worked as domestic servants and as agricultural labours. Padan Gochayat, son of Anand Gochayat, of the village belonging to the Dom caste served in a ship and visited several foreign countries. He came to the village for about three to four months in a year. The condition of the Doms, Bauris, Dhoba and Chamar was pitiable until the abolition of untouchability. The Dhobas are a highly useful group of people. They clean clothes and cut wood and carry it to the funeral ground in case someone died and was to be cremated.

Brahmins are, by nature and habit, reluctant to do hard physical labour though they do join agricultural work at different phases. No Brahmin tills land with plough and bullocks. These days, some take pleasure in tilling land with a power tiller and nobody takes it as a violation of the caste code. Brahmins join other caste people while separating the paddy plants from the wild growth in the field. Cutting of ripe paddy plant, for harvesting is not considered to be a derogation for the Brahmin. The Khandayats, as a caste are hardworking people and they specialize in agricultural activities. They get involved in the process right from the beginning and end up getting the yield stored properly in the Amara (specially built space for storage of food grains). Most of the other castes such as Gauda, (milk men), Dhoba (washer man), Bhandari (Barber), Bauri etc. besides following their caste occupation also work in the agriculture field.

The Chamars (toddy makers) spend their time in extracting toddy, marketing it and almost invariably, drinking it and getting thoroughly boozed. That made them, more or less, incapable of earning much and thus, they become poor. However, changes have come up in recent decades after some of them joined government jobs. A regular monthly income has facilitated improvement in their position.

The Doms play the drum during Hindu functions like marriage and Bratopanayan (sacred thread ceremony) of the Brahmins. They receive a paltry sum for this. They are allergic to agricultural labour. They specialize in going abroad in ships and earning good money which they lavishly spend in no time. The Doms, like other Harijans enjoy drinking toddy, the most common variety that the drink-lovers of this caste in the village consumed were palm toddy or Khajur toddy.

The Bauris are better than the Chamars and Doms in doing agricultural work. They prove reliable as domestic servants. We had many of them engaged as domestic servants on an annual basis. They moved freely in our house and were like family members.

Brahmins had access to learning right from the beginning. An ordinary Brahmin knows reading and writing and remembers Sanskrit slokas, mantras and purans because he lives on his priesthood. In course of time, the Brahmins had access to schools and colleges and as a result, they shifted from Sanskrit to English. They had the advantages of early English education and modernization as a consequence of it.

The dietary habits among the higher castes were more or less identical. Almost all such groups took meat and fish. I remember that none in our village from a

Brahmin family ate chicken. I took it first time in a friend's (Dandanirodh) house. The low castes did not care much for the type of food they took. Besides, eating what the higher caste people ate, they took pork, kochia, Genda, Samuka etc. Some of them also ate beef. This added to their un-cleanliness besides their qualification for un-touchability prior to 1947. Great changes have taken place after independence and the adoption of the constitution of India. The so-called low castes are now as respectable as the higher castes owing to their education, cleanliness and income.

Smoking was confined to the low caste and was regarded as a low caste behavior. However, some Khandayats smoked bidi. No Brahmin during our childhood days smoked a cigarette. We were given the impression that only bad people smoke and smoking was highly injurious to health and reputation. A cousin (maternal uncle's son) of mine somehow picked up the bad habit of smoking Bidi on his way back from the school. In nineteen hundred sixties, cigarette came to the village and many started smoking Scissors cigarettes, a popular brand then. Smoking started being viewed as a pattern of behaviour of the modern man.

The whiteness of the cigarette attracted many for a fun. I was no exception and one day, I smoked. Hardly did I take a puff in, I felt quite uncomfortable and was about to faint. During my days in Ravenshaw college, I saw some students smoking in order to remain awake at night to study in an undisturbed atmosphere. However, I never knew that ladies also smoked. I saw it for the first time in 1971 when a Lady Professor of the university smoked packets of cigarettes each day. It surprised me so much that I wrote to some friends about it.

The Scheduled Castes in the village

The scheduled caste people of the village have made remarkable progress in the last seven decades. These castes include the Doms, Bauris, Dhobas, Chamars, Keutas and Kandaras. Earlier, they lived in small slums outside the residential area of the high castes. The Doms and some Bauris lived in the North-Western side of the village. Some others lived in the Southern end of the village. Dhobas lived in the North-Eastern side. Close to their place of residence was a big tank where they could wash the clothes of the higher caste people. They received the annual remuneration in form of paddy besides some rice each time they washed the clothes. Kandaras were small in number and so also were the Keutas who got status of Scheduled Castes later, and as such, they lived inside the village. Their houses were very small thatched ones and the hygienic condition of their areas of settlements was quite deplorable. They had no access to safe drinking water. Later on, a well was specifically dug at their places to provide drinking water. The Doms prepared baskets out of bamboos and sold them for their livelihood. The Bauris waked as domestic servants for agricultural purpose besides working as agricultural labours. So were the Kandaras. Long back, they worked as security guards of the village and received some paltry remuneration. This practice has been discontinued since sixties.

The economic condition of each of these categories of people was pitiable. They were malnourished and poorly clothed and they were the poorest of the poor in the village. A few families of the Dom Sahi (their area of settlement was so called) worked in ships and visited some foreign lands. When they came back each year, they usually brought some expensive spices, perfumes, electronic goods such as radio, watch etc. and also some ready cash. During this period, they live a very comfortable life, take good food and also drink. They stay in the village for about four months and then leave the village to join their duties in ships. By the time they leave the village to rejoin work, they became paupers. Besides paying high rate of interest for the loan they take, they also gave preference to the loaner while disposing the foreign goods acquired by them.

To be precise, on most occasions, they had to depend upon begging and thus, they could not live a respectable life. Things have changed these days so significantly in respect of them that they are no less than others in the society. Thanks to the contribution of the schools (Village school and Sarada Academy of Kanakpur which provide education up to secondary level), colleges, the mass media and the antipoverty programs of state and the central governments.

Out of the sixteen Dom families, six have the houses built at their cost. Seven families availed housing grant under Indira Awas Yojana to construct their houses. Only three families continue to live in their thatched houses but the qualities of such thatched houses are much better. Five of these families possess motor cycles, one of them has a four-wheeler. All of them now have drinking water from the tube well. Of the six Dhoba families living on the North-Eastern side of the village, two have their own pucca houses and the remaining six have pucca houses given under the Indira Awas Yojana. There are 16 Bauri families in the village. Thirteen of them have pucca houses, two of which have been built at the cost of the family while the remaining 11 houses have been built under the Indira Awas Scheme. Five of the 16 families have motor cycle. Houses in all scheduled caste hamlets have electricity connection and provision for drinking water.

Kandara families are three in number and all of them have been awarded Indira Awas. One of them has built a house out of his own resources. Out of the five Chamar families, one has his own-built house though all of them have pucca houses under Indira Awas Yojana.

Among the scheduled caste people some have made remarkable progress, at least from the point of view of economic position. The Dom Sahi which was extremely dirty is now quite neat and clean. Padan Gochhayat who was the first among the Doms to go abroad had come with substantial amount of money and materials and could manage to put his own son Babaji in the said Profession. Babaji has acquired agricultural land, built his own pucca house, has all modern facilities of life (TV, Fridge etc.) and a motor cycle. Rangia Dom of yesteryears who was in abject poverty must be very happy to see his son Babaji who has built a very attractive building.

Nimain Gochhayat is a low-ranking government servant, he has a pucca house, his own tube well, T.V and a Motor Cycle. Besides, he has a four-wheeler. His son is a matriculate and his daughter-in-law is also a matriculate. His house is a model for his caste men. One thing remarkable among the scheduled caste people in the village is that they have now concentrated on their own development rather than wasting their time in moving from one place to another for nothing. Those of them who don't have much landed property, work as share croppers. This has helped them in living a good life.

Alekh Sethi (Dhoba) is a pensioner. His three sons (one- a truck driver, the second- a farmer and the third- owner of a cycle repair shop) have helped each other in having a pucca house of their own. From the point of view of education, the scheduled castes have not made much progress. None of them has gone beyond Matriculation. Had they acquired higher education, they would have done much better. These days, the scheduled castes cannot be ignored any more, particularly after their economic betterment and occupation of political office in the rural local government.

Land and Agriculture

Acquisitiveness is an inborn quality with man. He desires to acquire more and more of it. This becomes very strong where the land is productive. People in urban areas acquire land and sell it at a higher price or put it to some productive use. In the villages, people acquire land for several purposes; the most important among them being to add to their annual agricultural yield. In my village, the Chasas (agriculturists) were preoccupied mostly with land, agriculture and agriculture related problems (sowing seeds, preparing the plants, adding organic and chemical fertilizers, insecticides, the behaviour of the monsoon, cyclone, flood and their likely impacts).

Land, in the rural areas was always a factor for happiness or unhappiness. When acquired, it brings happiness and affluence to the family. In the same way, when it is lost, it amounts to loss of security and status in the community as also unhappiness to the family. When brothers in a family fight for their share in paternal property and the family land gets fragmented, it creates unhappiness in the minds of those who either purchased the land or derived pleasure in seeing the big size of the plot or the total extent of the land possessed by the family. Subdivision and fragmentation of the land adversely affects the yield in the land. Agricultural Reform enforced through settlement by the government have made some notable changes. These days fragmentation of land has become difficult, if not impossible.

Agriculture is a way of life requiring consistent hard work. Activities of the farmers are determined by agriculture. In some months of the year, the farmers have to give their fullest attention to farming operation. They have hardly any time to spare. In some months they are comparatively free. Irrespective of their castes, all farmers have to do, more or less, the same work at any given month. They carry the organic fertilizer to the land during April-May, plough the land and keep it ready for sowing seeds later. Earlier, rich land owners got the manures carried to the land either with the help of bullock-cart or by the engaged labourers. Small farmers carried these by themselves, Brahmin farmers, mostly, got it done through the paid labourers. The land had to be ploughed properly, twice (Do OD) or thrice (tin OD) depending on the nature of the soil and the efforts it needed to make it fit for sowing seed. This is mostly, done before sowing seeds which start on the 17th day of Baisakh, (in the month of May) known in 'Akshay Tritiya.'

Decades earlier, the farmers completed sowing of seeds by the second/third week of June because there was a good shower of rain almost each year on the Basumata Snan Day (the day of mother Earth's bath), falling between 14th and 17th of June each year. Weather change has disturbed the schedule now. These days, transplantation has become popular among the farmers. For this, the farmers prepare ground to grow and develop plants in a place with provision for water. Once the rain starts, the farmers lose no time in transplanting and thereafter applying doses of chemical and organic fertilizers as also pesticides as per needs in suitable intervals.

Floods, cyclones and droughts visit Odisha almost regularly at short intervals and add to the farmers' woes.

Investing good sum of money borrowed from Banks and losing the yields owing to such natural calamities breaks the economic backbone of the farmers.

The agricultural Workers

Both male and female workers are engaged in agricultural activities. A larger number of women workers come mostly from the scheduled castes. Compared to them, women workers from the touchable castes are less and still less from the Brahmin castes. If a Brahmin women had to work, she worked in her own field. Some male workers were hired as private and domestic servants on an annual basis. As I remember, they had a small remuneration ranging from Rs. 60/- to Rs. 100/- per annum. Some years later when the remuneration was raised to Rs.300/-, it was considered quite high. Daily wage of the agricultural worker in those days was a rupee per day for male workers and 12 annas (A Rupee one was equal to 16 annas) for female workers. Having seen them taking such differential wages from our father, we as children, played the game of labour where little girls played the role of women labour demanding wage equal to that of the male. Wage of the agricultural labour continued to be very low until Biju Patnaik, in his second term of chief Ministership in 1990 raised the minimum wage to Rupees twelve per day for both male and female workers. This was a revolutionary step.

Earlier, some large land owners allowed a poor family to cultivate and enjoy the benefits of some of their land and, in return, their whole family worked in the land owners farm. None in our village was such a big land owner. The maximum landed property, as I knew, was owned by Narshani Rout and the Pradhan families. None of them had more than 15 acres. Large land-owners had their servants and simultaneously, they employed daily labourers to work in their fields. This was particularly so in case of those who had more than one pair of bullock to draw the plough. My Bapa engaged two domestic servants (Jharia and Radha) along with some other wage labourers though he had only one pair of bullocks.

Adia Teli, the Oil man

While reading different newspapers on the abnormal price rise of edible oils, I thought how if we significantly reduce the use of edible oil and whether we can almost go without it. Besides economizing our family expenditure, it will act as a step against all diseases caused and facilitated by excess oil consumption. Thus, in course of my thinking, came a person before my mind's eye. He was a tall, bald and healthy man. He wore a dhoti (cloth). His head was wrapped with a gamucha. He was Adia Teli, (the oilman named Adia). Probably his name was Adikand, but people called him as Adia. I don't exactly remember the name of his village. I think he belonged to Khandasahi or Dandamar, the two villages situated at a distance of about 3km from ours. Once he reached the village, he shouted at the height of his voice "Khanti Sorish Tel" (Pure Mustard Oil), Ghanā Tel, Bhejāl nahin (no adulteration) etc. At a time, he carried a maximum of eight to ten seers of mustard oil in an earthen pot safely put in a small basket. He made a Pagdi with his gamucha, kept the basket on his head and moved from one village to another. He walked on foot to our village and from one end to the other. That was probably because he could not carry more oil at a time. It may also be because his Ghana could not extract more oil on a day.

Adia had a Ghana (an arrangement to extract oil from mustard seeds, ground nut seeds, coconut etc.) of his own. He claimed that the oil sold by him was pure and unadulterated. He was also believed by people who examined the purity of the oil by giving a touch of it at their nostril. Those days, there was limited scope for adulteration. The only oil which could be adulterated with the mustard oil was ground nut oil. It was not harmful. It is liked even now by many and in many parts of the country, it is the principal oil used in cooking. Besides cooking, the other purpose for which mustard oil was used was massaging.

We heard that high ranking officers, Zamindars and other rich men had the luxury of massage made by some peon/servant. For this purpose, mustard oil was used. In our village, people had no idea of such luxury. All that they did was to apply some mustard oil on their heads before taking bath. Applying oil in other parts of the body was limited to smaller number of people. Women used coconut oil to keep their hair in good condition. Men mostly, used mustard oil since coconut oil was costly. Coconut oil was used by most Brahmins since each one of the Brahmins families had some coconut trees. Non-Brahmin did not have coconut trees. It was said that if a non-Brahmin planted Nadia (Coconut), his homestead land would become podia (barren). This belief is no more there. Each coconut tree yielded at least 100 coconuts in a year. Extracting oil out of it was not difficult for them. I remember how our mother did that at home without taking these to the Ghana (Oil extractor) during my childhood. Oil extracting machines came later to villages.

People then, did not know the use of varieties of oil in cooking. Oil was not used for preparing all kinds of curries. Number of vegetables available in the market was limited. Almost all vegetable were season-specific. During the months of April to June, except the leafy vegetables (shag), other vegetables were not available. Tomato, Cabbage, Cauli flower etc. now available round the year, were available only during the winter. Potato was not popular nor was it always available. One seer of Potato was good enough for a family for a week.

While preparing curries, house-wives used a very small quantity of oil. Some vegetables were smoked in the chullah. There was no need to add oil to them. Fish and dry fish (Sukhua) were also smoked. Even when oil was used, its quantity was quite limited. In some cases, I have seen, some mustard seeds and red pepper were good enough as spices for preparing a curry. Jeera seeds were put on the hot handi and once the seeds give indication of having been duly fried, boiled vegetables were put into the hot handi. That made the curry tastey. On special occasions, my mother used coconut oil in preparing cakes, puri, kakara etc. Dalda came later and still later came large number of unhealthy oils.

The price of Ghana tel was less than one rupee per seer. Yet, people mostly purchased one, two or maximum four chataks of oil at a time. Eight chataks was good enough for a family for a month. I remember my mother sometimes went beyond eight chataks in a month. In no case the family consumed more than one seer of oil in a month. One seer was equal to 16 chataks. Adia Teli had devised his own instrument, made from bamboo of different sizes to measure oil. Introduction of metric system of measurement resulted in people demanding oil as per that. Seer was replaced by kiloliter in 1956-57. Ghanas became inoperative and the Adia telis disappeared from the villages. People had oil from shops.

With availability of different brands of oil in the competitive market, adulteration, has become a regular nuisance. People now search for Ghana tel and new

Adia telis some times are noticed in villages and lanes of Bhubaneswar.

Village Life:

Clothes people wore: Brahmins wore dhoti below the waist and draped a gamucha (country towel) on the shoulder. Sometimes, they managed with a gamucha or a lungi. Conservative Brahmins did not approve wearing a lungi. However, this has now been accepted among the younger generation. They also put on trousers and shirts. Brahmins of sixties of the last century in our village did not go beyond a banian or a shirt in addition to a dhoti if they went outside the village. Except those who were working in some government office, no Brahmin, then, had even a pair of Chappals. The Khandayats usually managed with a dhoti and Gamucha (if well off) or a lungi or even a gamucha in the day-to-day life. In case they went out, they also had a banian or a shirt. As far as I have seen, despite some being well off and economically better off than others, food and dress in the village did not make much difference among families.

Pan: An item for good will: Pan played a very important of part in receiving guests in the village. The women, usually, prepare the pan for every one's consumption, especially for the elders like father-in-law and mother-in-law. Outsiders from the village as also guest from other villages were offered Pan as a gesture of courtesy. Preparation of this item consists of placing lime on the pan leaf, smearing catechu on a small stick and putting in necessary amount of spice (like elaichi, labanga) and pile them and keep them under the cover of a piece of moist cloth. These days, these piles of Pans are being put in stainless steel container in some families. High Government officials also carry pan in steel containers while going to office. It is also an act of courtesy to offer pan to a visitor.

Cooking, Fuel and the Kitchen: Cooking food for the family was the main duty of the women members. It was considered as a female act and, if some males did it, they were criticized as womanish. The housewives cooked food, mostly twice a day (at mid-day for lunch and, in the evening, for the dinner). Male members were mostly busy in the fields for the whole year in agricultural operations. Some women, mainly, from the lower economic background, worked in agriculture, in their own land and as labourer in others' field. Yet, cooking was a business of the women. The food cooked by them both for lunch and dinner mainly included rice, dal or Alu chatni. Wheat was not a part of staple food in Odisha in general and rural Odisha in particular till sixties. It was the elderly people or the sick who took chapati. Some people viewed consumption of chapati as an indication that the said consumer did not have adequate rice. Even in late seventies, I know a particular Engineer from a rich agricultural family (who retired in very high rank) who said that those who did not have adequate rice, wheat came to their rescue. Chapati was also not much known. We saw it in hotels at Kanakpur in our school days. Earthen pots, known as Handi, were used in the Kitchen. (called Handishal).

The fuel used in the kitchen included dry leaves of trees and some pieces of dry cowdung (called Gunda) and round shaped cow dung cake (called Ghasi). Fire wood was not available to all. It was a privilege of the well to do families which had trees on their own land. Those who had purchasing power, they could purchase trees, cut them into pieces, dry them and use them. Those who had neither their own trees nor had they the necessary purchasing power, they had to manage with cow dung cakes or dry leaves of trees. Some of them collected dry branches of trees standing on government land outside the village and used these as fuel. Some months of a year (say from March to June) did not cause any problem of collecting fuel. The needy people went out of the village, collected dry branches of trees, dry leaves, cow dung from the village grazing ground and prepared fuel out of these. During the rainy season, they found it difficult to gather fuel. Some prepared extra cow dung cakes during summer to use them during the rains. Cowdung cakes are sold as fuel even these days.

Among the trees which were suitable for the purpose of being used as firewood were Chakunda, Banyan, Mango, Jackfruit, Coconut etc. Unless coconut trees and mango trees, stopped bearing fruits, these were not cut for the purpose of getting fire wood. Chakunda was most suitable for firewood purpose. One could cut the whole tree or a few branches only. These branches were cut to small piece which would conveniently be put into the Chulla. There were special shades built to preserve the fire wood. We did not have many trees of our own and had to purchase a tree as a whole, and make it suitable for use.

Even when we cut trees for the purpose of getting fuel, we normally, cut only a few branches, not the whole tree. On rare occasions, a tree in full was felled. Scope for further growth and use in future was always a point that deserved consideration.

Many, during those days, could not afford to purchase a match box to light the fire in the kitchen although the cost was very small. Often housewives from our neighborhood came twice to our house to collect fire for their kitchen. Since caste system was rigid, my mother brought out some fire from the Chullah and gave it to those who came for it. They were not allowed to take it directly from our challah.

In the last seven decades village life has undergone unbelievable change. No more people depend upon dried leaves for their cooking fuel. Nobody these days, not even people belonging to Scheduled Caste community cook food on the earthen chullah. Every one's Kitchen and kitchen inventories have changed significantly. More than 75% of the villagers have gas Chullah and modern utensils. Quite a few have crockeries and varieties of plates, saucers and such other materials. Two gas distributing companies (HP and Indane) have opened their distribution centres not far from our village (i.e. at Tirtol and Jagannathpur). Home delivery of gas cylinders is made within 24 hours of registration by the consumer. Earthen Handis are now replaced by stainless steel or Aluminium Handis. Some people, in the village have modular kitchens.

The village which was an example of educational backwardness and poverty is now a totally different one. As has been noticed during the study of the village, some of those who, during their lifetime, could hardly get two square meals a day, would be extremely happy if they became alive to see their children and grandchildren owning motor cars, bikes, pucca houses, washing machine, refrigerator, T.V. etc. Even one from among the Scheduled Caste (Dom) owns a four-wheeler, a Bike and a pucca house. One whose father was a primary school teacher and had a very small extent of landed property, now has two buildings, four bikes, a car, a tube well, Refrigerator, T.V. and a Washing Machine. Another school teacher who educated his sons, is now owner of a Car, Bikes, Cycle and a Laptop. This is a nice example of development in the village. So also, is the case of a scheduled caste person who is one of the very affluent persons of the village. A village where electricity was a dream, now has uninterrupted electricity supply. In some houses, quite a large number of the families use inverters in the village.

Dhenki and Dhenkisal: One thing which posed problems before the housewives in the village was preparation of the grains for use in cooking food. In Odishan villages, rice was the principal food (in fact, the only food) till early sixties. Subsequently, people chose to eat wheat for several reasons including its easy availability in the rural areas. Ragi was also consumed in Odisha but it was mostly confined to the poor segments of the population who could not produce adequate paddy for their family consumption. Making paddy and ragi fit for cooking was the responsibility of the housewives. De-husking the paddy was done in two phases and ultimately the husks were removed with the help of a primitive pestle and mortar (Known as Dhenki). A hole of suitable size dug out of a block of iron served for mortar. This was embedded in a floor and about a five feet long stout wooden pole, with an iron band at either end, served for the pestle. Two women worked the pestle while the third had to mind the mortar. The two women who worked the pestle were mostly from lower but touchable castes or were poor. Such women were pejoratively, called Dhan Kutuni (the paddy de-huskers). However, such women were not allowed by Brahmins to do this work if the rice to be de-husked was to be used for puja, preparation of prasad or use in pitru shradh. In such a case, women of the family or these from the Brahmin caste had to do it.

Mati Handi, Handishal, Rosai (Earthern Containers, Kitchen and Cooking): Handi refers to a utensil or container and Mati Handi means an earthen container manufactured by a special group of people named as Kumbhar or Kumbhakar. These Handis were of different sizes and shapes depending upon the purpose for which these were used. These had a variety of uses. One of such uses was in cooking food. For a standard family in the village, there was a special place in the kitchen called a 'Tengeda' (a heightened earthen alter of about 3 feet long). There were, on it, three holes on which three Handis could be placed in a stable condition. There was another small Tengadi with a hole on it. A Mathia (earthen pot) would be finally kept on it. For a Brahimin family, the Handishal (kitchen) was a sacred place and the sanctity of food and water kept in the Handishal was of vital consideration. It is believed that the forefathers visit the house at night and take food and water available in the Handisal for them. Therefore, Brahmin housewives always keep some food and drink for them in the Handishal. Thus, the sanctity and purity of food, drink and that of the Handishal was of enormous importance. My mother said, besides this, the justification for keeping food and drink available in the Handishal at night was also to meet the situation in case some Atithi (guest) reached at odd hours and needed food. Inside the Handishal was a special Chullah where food offerings were cooked on the Pitrushradha day. The Handishal assumes special importable when a new daughter-in-law, coming for the first time after her marriage, falls prostrate in the Handishal and performs her puja before cooking the first meal in the in-law's place.

As a matter of principle, no non-vegetarian food was cooked in the Handishal. In case, some members took non-vegetarian food, it was cooked outside. Entry into Handishal was restricted to caste people only. In case a dog got into the Handishal, it was considered in-auspicious and all the Handis and food contained therein were thrown out. The Handishal was purified, puja was performed and a new set of Handis was brought in replacing the old ones. Each day, the Handis were cleaned with the help of dried paddy leaves. Pakhal (soaked rice) prepared in Mati Handi had a distinct flavor. Besides rice dal and varieties of curries, the other preferred food (like Khiri and cakes) was cooked in Mati Handi.

Another special item was a milk product. When milk was boiled well for a long duration in slow heat using cow dung cake as the fuel, the water content in the milk got reduced and the boiling milk changes its colour to light brown from white. Such milk was very tasteful. When the milk is further boiled with sugar to a semi solid state, it is called Rabidi, a delicious sweetmeat. Even after the Rabidi is taken out, some solid parts of it (which is slightly burnt) still remain stuck to the container. These are removed before the container is cleaned. This remaining part of the Rabidi is called the Koru. We loved it more than we loved milk. The ghee prepared in the Mati Handi had an excellent flavour and taste. Sixties of the last century started replacements of these Mati Hndis by those made of Aluminium or stainless steel. The new utensils were convenient to handle and the housewives did not always have to clean them every day. Besides, there was no apprehension of their being broken. In rural Odisha, by the late eighties, almost all Mati Handis were replaced by Aluminium Handis. On ceremonial occasions such as marriages, upanayans and other types of puja, Mati Handi continues being used as a symbol.

Pal Bhoot (Dried Paddy plant ghost): During the Dushera, young boys of the village made several types of merrymaking. These were done in the evening hours. Some played cards, some played Kaudi, arrange opera show and Pal Bhoot (dried paddy plant ghost). Pal Bhoot was the most entertaining among them. This was done by boys only. Equally enjoyable was the Dal Bhoot (Branch ghost). In this case, small branches of trees and leaves cover the body of the boy who acts as Bhoot (ghost). During the night of Kumar Purnami (full-moon night of Ashwin), these Bhoots moved from one place to another in the village, some enjoyed it and some got frightened at the sight of these so-called ghosts. Some naughty boys tried to frighten the girls who played in groups in the moonlit nights. However, this was a type of merry making and it has now gradually got out of sight; particularly after electrification of the village.

I remember one occasion when one of our age (Tima) became a Pal Bhoot and danced so much before the girls playing Puchhi that they loudly raised a cry for help. Guardians and other senior persons came out of their houses. They reprimanded Tima and cautioned him not to repeat this in future. These days, special programmes in the T.V. on the occasion of Kumarotsav have become so elaborate and entertaining that nobody likes going out for Palabhoota.

Some bases of rural conflict

No society can ever be free from conflict. My village was no exception. When I try to understand the nature of rural conflict in my village, I see a pattern. In our days the conflicts within the village were limited to mostly four major types.

(1) The Hido Hana conflict (Ridge trimming conflict): Village life was land directed and land oriented. Possession of land was a matter of honour and the life of people was directed by achievements from land. There was a quest for

more and more land. It was central to both happiness and suffering in the village. It brought happiness and prestige to the family when new plots of land were added to its stock of land.

Land also was the cause of tension and unhappiness when big and reputed families broke, brothers were separated, land was distributed or sold. Brothers sometimes fought amongst themselves for their share of parental and ancestral property in the village and also in the courts. One of the common grounds on which people in the village quarrelled was proper maintenance of Hido (ridges). In case of the agricultural lands, one plot is different from the other from the point of view of its ownership, size and record details. Every year, before the transplantation of the plant, the ridges separating one plot from another are trimmed as a part of the process to make the field ready for agricultural operation. Owners of each side of the plot are expected to carefully trim their sides without affecting the size of the adjacent plot. Some, however, do not do so. This leads to conflict, physical assault, violence and ultimately court cases. So also, happens in case of some brothers who partition parental property and are separated. Sometimes, such conflict leads to violence and murder.

(2) *Planting trees:* Some trees have very luxuriant growth. Such trees grow very fast and sprout branches in all directions in such a way that they cover a good extent of land and make it unprofitable and unfit for cultivation. Notorious elements in the village, in their scheme to grab their adjacent plots, plant such trees at the extreme end of their plot. In no time, such trees (mostly Chakunda), make the targeted plot unprofitable to its owners. Thus begins his complaint, his approach to the village, elders or forcefully cutting it and involving himself in violence, F.I.R. and Court

cases. Sometimes such trees are planted in homestead areas to cause strain and tension (in case of cyclone) in the neighbouring families. We had an experience of such type. A plot adjacent to our homestead land (more particularly to the building) had a tamarind tree which is believed to be quite inauspicious. Besides, the tree spread over our homestead land and almost touched the house. Several requests to the concerned neighbour to remove the tree or to cut the spreading branches did not yield any result. The matter went to the court and ultimately, the cyclone of 1999 solved it.

(3) *Crop damage:* Another cause of conflict in the village relates to damage of crops caused by domestic animals such as buffalos, cows etc. let loose by their owners or managers. The cattle go out for grazing in the open fields reserved as gochara (cattle grazing ground). A care-taker or manager (called Gayal) is engaged by the villagers to take the cattle to be gochara and bring them back in the evening. It thus, becomes the responsibility of the Gayal to ensure that the cattle do not enter the crop fields and the crops of the farms are left unaffected. Sometimes, they fail to do that and the cattle cause damage to crops. The affected farmer takes the Gayal and the cattle owner to task. Sometimes, cattle of some particular people, almost as a habit, get in to particular plot and damage the crops. This leads to bad blood and generation of conflict. Quite often, it is neither the cattle owner nor the Gayal who is really guilty. The particular cow or bullock is a rogue among the group and gets into the crop field and creates undesirable situation.

(4)*Village money lenders:* Some scholars of social sciences who have made village studies have found out that the scheming village money lenders usurp the land of others, particularly when they advance some loan to some of them. Such money lenders normally take signature of the loanee on the blank page and prepare the document later to their advantage. The land entered in the documents is grabbed by them if the loanee fails to pay back in time. This causes great distress for the victim and results in conflicts of different types. Fortunately for our village, as far as I know, there was no such loaner. These days, most of these problems have been addressed by the government as a result of the Land Reform, prevention of fragmentation of holdings and easy loan available through Banks.

Unproductive Indebtedness

Generation of surplus removes poverty and therefore, people in the village avail loans from cooperative Banks and commercial Banks to take up such measures as would facilitate surplus generation. Loans are received for land development, starting business, adding to efficiency in work, purchase of seeds and fertilizers, purchase of bullocks, milch cows, opening of shops etc. Land development promotes yield, production of seeds of good quality and use of fertilizers. Therefore, those who make proper use of these loans in agricultural development, or purchase power tiller and make use of it in their own field and/or hire it out for other people's use, purchase good quality seeds and adequate fertilizer for use in agriculture, etc. succeed in creating surplus in their income which, in course of time, is utilized as capital for further production. Indebtedness ends, in such cases, with capital formation and betterment in the condition of the farmer. Such cases of indebtedness may be called productive indebtedness. However, in quite a large number of cases in the village, indebtedness becomes unproductive when the loan money is put to unproductive uses.

In our childhood days, loans from the Banks were

quite rare. Banks started involving themselves mostly after nationalization of 14 commercial Banks in 1969. Earlier people availed themselves of loans mostly from cooperatives and village money lenders against which, the latter took land, ornaments and some such valuable assets on mortgage for a fixed period. The rates of interest were quite high, sometimes one anna (6 paise) for a rupee per month. In case the poor farmer failed to repay the loans, the money lender grabbed the mortgaged land or asset and the farmer moved from pillar to post to get back his asset and ultimately failed. Sometime, the poor borrowed paddy from the rich in the village and, to repay the debt, he mortgaged some particular plot of paddy. The total product from that plot went to the paddy lender. Things have remarkably changed though every year Odisha suffers from the scandals of farmers committing suicide owing to crop failure. Recently, new schemes have been introduced by the Government of Odisha and that of India to come to the rescue of the farmer. Poverty eradication program and those of employment guarantee schemes have facilitated improvement in the life of the village poor.

Condition of the farmer could have been much better had the loanee been conscious and responsible in utilizing the loan money judiciously and had the officials involved in operating the system been fair and honest. Unfortunately, some loanees misuse the loan money in diverting it to unproductive uses (daughter's marriage, parental death rites, purchase of unproductive assets and some time for a lavish life). Vagaries of monsoon also add to this. Recently, the state government has started a program of rural agricultural development, popularly Known as KALIA, which besides giving cash to the farmers to purchase seed, fertilizer etc, also provides scholarships to the school and college going children of the village poor. This program may help developing human resource besides helping generation of surplus. It seems to be a well considered decision.

A point on which some strict action through enactment is necessary is to minimize rural indebtedness. There should be no compromise. Marriage expenses should be minimized in imposing limits on guests, celebration and gifts presented to the daughter and son-in-law. Once people become conscious of these unproductive expenditure vis-à-vis their own financial position, there will be no need of the Act or its enforcement by the authorities.

I know some cases of people selling their land, bullocks, milch cows and ornaments to spend in observing parental death rites or celebrating marriages in the family. I remember my adoptive father expired in 1990 and we had to offer feasts to other Brahmins of our own village and from some other villages for four days (5th, 7th, 9th and 12th days of the death of him).

Some Brahmins in the village, sometimes, take advantage of the financial difficulties of the mourning families in forcing arrangement of a lavish feast. The mourning family in some cases mortgages or sells land and other assets to meet the expenditure. On the death of my adoptive father, one greedy Brahmin came to express condolences to me. In course of informal discussion, my father narrated our plan of observance and casually asked him if it was alright. He seemed to have waited for such an occasion and replied "all village elders may be invited to plan things and items". My father retorted "Why, I am older than the so-called elders, nobody ever asked me about it in the past. Why should I ask anybody? We will arrange as per the tradition, decide the total number of guests to be invited and the items to be served. I am sure it would be alright". That actually happened and all, including this one, attended the feasts. This shows how one should decide his case as per his position and sweet will. To feed people on such occasions is alright and we also believe in the philosophy behind this tradition. We must decide as per our abilities. There should be no compulsion in this.

Such demand for feasts is not peculiar to Brahmins only. This also happens for other caste people too. The poor are compelled to offer Bhoji (Feast) on the occasions of marriage and death in the family. Some find it almost impossible to give the daughter in marriage. The caste groups demand Bhai Bhat (Community feast). Those who do not obey the command of the Bhai (Community) are punished- the family is boycotted. Our village had almost no such cases.

Bhadra lok, Bhal lok and Tout

I remember a small group of persons (about 5 to 10) was always readily available to advise the common villagers in their hours of crisis. They settled disputes arising among the villagers. They had a key role in amicably settling problems of partition among brothers. They were called Bhadra lok or Bhal lok (gentlemen or good men). Some of them were really so but some were otherwise. Instead of settling disputes, they engineered crises for some good and happy families. When it came for them to sit as judge in the dispute, their honesty and impartiality quickly disappeared. Their activities were limited mostly to the village. Occasionally, some of them went to the office of the Sub Registrar when some land was sold or purchased or transferred. Two Brahmins (X. Dash and Y. Dash) were engaged doing this business. Unaware, people contacted them both for purchase and sale of land and the Bhadraloks came forward in getting the deal done. Sometimes, one of them worked on behalf of the seller and the other one represented the case of the purchaser.

The seller engages the Bhadralok for a good price while the purchaser seeks help for a favourable price. All had to approach them for the details of the land, its naxa (map) and such other technical questions. Naxa of land, of all in the village were available with these persons and it became an instrument for earning good income for both of them. Such mediators were thoroughly familiar with the village map. In case there was any dispute (such disputes were frequent), measurement of the accuracy of the plots was done and for this, the Naxa was obtained from these the so called Bhadraloks at a cost.

Cultural Activities in the Village

Annual Drama: Young boys of the village studying in the schools and colleges met for a long duration during the summer. They planned some programme such as, visiting Goddess Sarala, organizing feast, enacting a drama etc. for common enjoyment in the village. In early sixties, such an effort was made and a Drama Society was constituted. Late Purna Ch. Dash was the guiding spirit in this connection. Purna Babu (Popularly referred to as Purna Bhaina) was the mentor and he provided direction in acting. He also did the important business of prompting at the stage. We decided to have a drama only by male members.

The actors were from the village. Only one (Padma Ch. Mohanty alias Padan) was from the neighbouring village (Khandtang). The actors were Bibu (Bijay Krishna Swain), Biju (Bijaya K Nanda), Seson (Subas Ch. Dash), Prema, Parava etc. Brundaban Dash (Buna Bhaina as he is known) also kept awake till late at night to provide guidance in acting. The practice was done in the house of Mishras kept under the supervision of Shib Ch. Dash.

The venue of the stage was a critical question to solve. Where to have it? Inside the village or outside near the school? We did it once near the village school in the Padma Pokhari Shamshan. Next year, it was located inside the village despite the road (Dānda) inside the village being narrow. Women and girls did not find it convenient to go out of the village at night to witness the drama. They asked the organisers to change the venue. Besides, staging it out side was much costlier which we found was difficult to afford. Therefore, the venue of the stage was in the middle of the village. It was in front of the Dash Sahi (in front of the houses of the Dash families) where the village road was comparatively wider and it could accommodate a larger number of viewers.

Resource mobilization was a real problem. The villages people were rather quite good to us. They had love for us since we were good boys in their estimate. Some of them contributed labour in collecting bamboos, constructing the pandal, stitching the screens, samiana etc. Besides, they also donated funds for it.

Electricity in the village was beyond our comprehension then. We had to procure a few petromax lights and Day- Lights (as they were called). Some times, the kerosene was donated by the shop keepers of the village. The whole business was more or less on a cooperative basis. I remember the plays performed were 'Chakri' in one year and 'Karnarjun' the next year. I acted in both the plays. So did Biju, Bibu and Padan. The most important roles were played by me and Biju in both the shows.

Every year, following the drama, there was a feast. The actors and all those directly associated with the drama participated in it. The feast was quite simple, we had only two items (rice and mutton curry). During the sixties, wine started gradually gaining access to rural areas. We restrained ourselves from any such drink (not even Bhang). As far as I know, all of us scrupulously adhered to our oath to be te-to-taller in career. This in fact, was a contribution of Purna mastre who added to our cultural foundation in creating a desire to be a proud te-to-taller.

There was an interesting experience. The day we staged the drama in Padma Dānda, we started rather late to enable people to come after their dinner at about 8.00 pm. The drama continued for about 3 hours and by the time it was over, we were thoroughly exhausted. However, the screens, the Samina and tarpaulin etc. were to be dismantled as most of these were received with the promise to return them in the next morning. We decided not to go home. We slept under the Samiana not far from the Shamshan (funeral ground) where hundreds of ghosts and witches were believed to be moving in the night. This was an unforgettable experience. We were happy in the morning to discover that we had no problem despite the ghosts.

Educational Facilities

Lower Primary to High School: Govindpur Lower Primary School (LPS) was one of the earliest of such institutions in Cuttack (now Jagatsinghpur) district. Its exact date of establishment is not traceable. However, based on certain objective calculations (record of its earliest students) it can be said that it came to exist, latest, sometime in the second decade of the 20th century. This school catered to needs of the village and those of the group of neighbouring villages. It had also some students from far off villages. One such example was Bhagaban Mohanty of the village BARTOL, (at a distance of about 20 KMs).

Bartol is a sea side village and the little boy (a classmate of my brother (94) stayed in a relations family to have his education. The house accommodating the school was a big hall. It was partitioned in the middle. The walls were made of bricks and cement and the floor was partly pucca. Tin sheets covered the hall. There were two big windows on both the Northern and Southern sides but there were no doors fitted to any of these windows. There was no Black Board which we saw when we joined Class-IV of Sarada Academy, Kanakpur in 1953.

There were two teachers in the school. They were Padma Charan Mohanty (Head Pandit) and Purna Charan Swain (Assistant Pandit). They were popularly referred to as Bada Master and San Master respectively. Two others, Banamali Parija and Madan Mohan Nanda served in the school for a short duration.

Padma Charan Mohanty and Purna Chandra Swain worked in the school for about 3 decades. They were, in fact, the two persons who laid the foundation for education and development in Govindpur and its adjoining area. Teaching students of pre-school class (Shishu Sreni) and Class-I was San Master's business. Bada Mastre taught students of classes II and III. San Mastre motivated students in many positive ways – he told stories of great national heroes and saints and he tried to lay the cultural foundation of Odisha and India in the heart of Students. Himself a devotee of Ramakrishna Paramhans Dev, he told stories on Ramakrishna and other saints. His handwriting was very beautiful and he helped us improve our handwriting by regular practice. Good manners and cleanliness were the two points he emphasized. He was loving and yet, a strict disciplinarian. He used the canes to curb naughty and deviant pupils.

Bada master had a very grave personality. He

was very strict in matters of discipline. He made students memorise things from the text book. All students were scared of him. He taught Arithmetic along with other subjects. He had very careful eyes on both bright and dull students. Both the teachers were fountains of love for the students despite the punishment they awarded to the deviants.

San Mastre was himself a freedom fighter who spent some time in jail. He spoke on Gandhi and the freedom movements to us. He also sang some of the popular songs of the freedom fighters.

Unlike these days, the LP Schools did not have any peon or sweeper to clean the floor. It was done by students. The girl students of class –II and III did it. We also some times did it on rotation basis. Nobody, then, made any complaint before any authority if his son / daughter was asked by the teacher to do this work. Also, both boys and girls worked in the garden developed in the school. We had different varieties of flower plants and we grew some vegetables like garlic, cabbage, tomato, Brinjal and some variety of shag (leafy vegetables).

Education beyond L.P. Level: Having education beyond LP level was a problem for many. The girls were the immediate victims. There was an M.E. school at Kanakpur and another at Tirtol. Going to Tirtol was difficult because of the river and lack of road communication. For education beyond primary level, students preferred Kanakpur M.E. School. My Bhaina too had his middle school education at Kanakpur. For high school education, Bhaina had to go to Korua although a high school was also started at Kanakpur in the name of Sarada Academy in the same year. M.S. Academy Tirtol came up in 1944. Padmanav Nanda who was senior to Bhaina and probably the first matriculate of the village had his education at B.B. High School, Kujang. I took admission in Class-IV in 1953. By this time, the Sarada Academy Kanakpur provided teaching in class IV to class XI. To some extent, it became convenient for students (both boys and girls) to have education up to matriculation.

Upgradation of Village L.P. School: It was owing to the care of the then local MLA (Basant Biswal) that this school was upgraded to M.E. level. A private High School (Swami Vivekananda High School) was formed in 1979. The school started getting grant-in-aid in March 1987. Since June, 1994, it has become a full-fledged government school. The Head Master of the school has both the M.E and High School under his administrative control. The school has now teachers for all levels from primary to High School.

As regards education beyond matriculation, the problem no more exists. There are +2 and +3 Colleges at Tirtol, Rahama and Kujanga. As a result, more and more lady students take admission in these colleges and the level of female education has risen. Quite a good percentage of girls of the village are now college educated and some of them have taken up government or private jobs.

Swami Vivekananda High School

The Two Teachers of Govindpur Primary School: I valued the two teachers of the Primary School (Head Pandit Padma Ch. Mohanty and Asstt. Teacher Purna Chandra Swain) very high in view of their excellent teaching, love and the care they took of the students besides being good role models before them. Both of them taught well and often tried to instill moral ideas into the minds of the students. Stories from great sages and statesmen were so nicely told by them that these had tremendous impact on us in our day-to-day life. Both of them had always an eye on me since they loved me and wished me well. Since ours was the only primary school in that area, students from other neighboring villages were with us. In fact, one can reasonably say that most of the subsequent developments in these villages were the outcome of these two teachers' contributions. Long after their retirement, when I was awarded the degree of Ph D from Berhampur university. I met Sri Mohanty who embraced me and put his hand on my head and said, "Ma Sarala Tote Bahut Krupa Karantu" (May Goddess Sarala shower blessings on you). Sri Purna Chandra Swain's house in the village was close to that of ours and I was very close to him and had his blessing always. Both of these great gurus are no more.

Purna Chandra Swain, popularly called Purna mastre was a follower of Ramakrishna Paramahansa and he had a lot of experience with the saints of the Ashram. He told us stories relating to the Sadhus and their spiritual experiences. He had the habit of explaining thing as per Ramakrishna's Philosophy. Purna Mastre had another creditable background. He was a freedom fighter and was jailed for this. People said that when police arrested him for his role in freedom struggle, he was beaten mercilessly. To each blow on his body by the police, his response was

Bharat Mata ki Jai. We were very much inspired to know this. He kept all details about me and wished me well. The last when I came to meet him and have his blessings was in 2007. He was an ideal person.

Health Care in the Village

In our childhood days, people in the village depended on a Homeopathic doctor in case of any illness. The Homeopaths, I am afraid, had no formal education in homeopathy. The doctor who visited the village, on call (in a Cycle) was Nimain Babu (Nimain Ch. Parija) of the village Tentulipada. He carried a box, out of it he gave us medicine. He claimed visit fee and medicine cost. If I remember correctly, the total due came to about one rupee. Sometimes, people made part payment owing to their inability to pay one rupee at a time. There was another Homeopath (Gouri Shyam Das) at Kanakpur. He was said to be a more competent homeopath. Both the homeopaths wore Khadi cloth and Khadi Punjabi. Our neighbour, the first pensioner of our village (Brundaban Swain), was under the treatment of Gourishyam Das of Kanakpur and he made it a point to send details about his health each day to Gouri Babu. My brother (Ranga bhai) was his messenger who gave details of his illness to the doctor and carried the medicine from him. Each day he became late in school because of this old man (we called him Ajaa). Brundaban Ajaa worried him every day to such an extent that he tried to avoid him. My father, however, advised him strictly not to disrespect the grand old man who had his blessings for us.

Towards the end of 1950's, an L.M.P. doctor (Dr Hari Charan Das) opened his clinic in the Kanakpur bazaar. He was an impressionable person and he moved on a green model Raleigh Cycle. People consulted Hari Babu and paid him higher amount of money. Hari Babu also visited the patient's house and demanded a fee which only a few could afford to pay.

There was an Allopathic hospital at Manijanga; a village at a distance of about 10 Kilometers from our village. It was a government hospital and it had an MBBS doctor and a nurse and other members of staff. All the preliminary treatment was made in this Hospital. Since there was no specialist available in the Hospital, serious and complicated cases were referred to the SCB Medical College Hospital, Cuttack. Those who could afford to spend for it went to Cuttack for treatment.

Many in our area could not take the benefit of the government Hospital of Manijanga. These included old people and expectant mothers. There was no conveyance available to carry them to Manijunga. The only mode of conveyance was a bullock cart. Between the village and Manijanga flows a river which, because of flood each year, prevented movement of any conveyance. As a result, people had to depend on homeopathic treatment. Some uneducated and untrained poor women had to do the midwifery. These unskilled women were from lower socioeconomic groups. They helped in child delivery. In quite a number of cases, either the child or the mother or both died owing to wrong methods adopted by the village midwife.

These days, thing have changed a lot. People have become health care conscious and the state is also extending possible assistance for nutrition as also growth and delivery of the child. The expectant mothers have frequent health checks and medical counsel. In our village, there are three qualified doctors and, at Kanakpur, there are some health clinics. The Manijanga Hospital in now a much bigger Hospital with specialists in different branches of treatment. Modes of conveyance have multiplied. The village is no longer inaccessible, there are roads from the village connecting to all places. The river that stood on the way of a patient's movement to Manijanga is no longer so because of the bridge over it and the pucca road connecting the village with Manijanga. Taxi, bus, autorickshaw, cycle rickshaw and also Ambulance carry patients each day at any hour. In the village itself, at Padma Dānda, there is a Public Health Clinic. People have become health conscious because of the rapid educational advance and the role played by mass communication.

Some Notable Village Elders

Some of the elders in the village seemed notable to me at different phases of life. Each one of them was prominent in one or other areas of activities in village life. One such persons was Brindaban Swain who was the first pensioner in our village. He had a good personality with his royal moustache and spectacles. He looked grave and was soft- spoken to children. He had an orange tree and he obliged me with an orange when I approached him. His voice was full of affection, yet some people were afraid of him. He would ask a question and if one could give a satisfactory answer, he would give oranges.

There was another person Balakrishna Swain alias Bali Swami. He was of very fair complexion and had a very big tummy which, he said, contained a cart- load of rice, dal and fish curry. Consumption of pan made his lips dark red and he looked quite like a Bhima of Mahabharat. He was full of love to me in view of my mother being the daughter of his friend. His wife Chitri Aai (Chitrangada) was quite good to me and gave me oranges and guavas when I asked her.

Fakir Muduli was another notable person in the

village – He was tall, stout, vocal and black. His moustache was different from all others. He had a goat farm which had more than 50 goats. These goats were well bred and, during the Rajo celebrated in June every year, about 15 to 25 of his goats were killed to provide mutton to different families. Mutton, then, was very cheap, rupee one was good enough for about one kilogram. I remember to have gone there to bring mutton from his place. We got mutton of rupees two on each of the two days. However, we were not allowed to go to the place where the goats were butchered.

Fakir Muduli was a courageous person and he never spared a word to anybody. He was forthright and indomitable. My father called him Fakir Bhai and he lovingly addressed me as Shashur (father-in-law). Once there was a case of corruption by a contractor who was entrusted with the work of reclamation of the village tank (Padma Pokhari). People complained before the authorities and an enquiry was undertaken. In presence of the villagers (mostly uneducated and particularly in English) the officer used English word while talking to the contractor. The villagers felt that enquiry should be in Odia and not in English. When the contractor and the Enquiry officer repeated talks in English, Fakir Stood up and said "why do you ask question in English?" Let us know the questions and the answers. Then alone you will know the truth from us". When they repeated talking in English, Fakir Shouted, "*Tum Chor ka Bhai Galkata*". All of us, as students of the school on the bank of Padma Pokhari were frightened.

There was another person Chintamani Pradhan, a rich farmer, well behaved and very nice to talk to. He wore a clean dhoti and a banian. The important point about him was that he was a very close friend of my mother's father Chakradhar Dash and both of them visited our house at least 3 to 4 times each month. Whenever some good and tasty food came to our house, my mother called for both of them and they had their share of food earlier than we had. He was believed to be a gentleman and people respected his views on village matters.

When I think of my village or I visit it, the first person who comes to my mind is Kanduri Swain. He was a role model for me in many ways. He was not a highly educated person nor was he a rich man possessing enormous quantity of wealth. He was a farmer, not a big one, his family included himself and his wife. His income certainly was not high, he himself worked in the field and earned his living therefrom. His clothes included a lungi, gamcha and a chadar, but sometimes when he visited goddess Sarala or went to Kanakpur hat (market) he wore a dhoti and a banian or shirt. However, these clothes were neat and clean as much as his body though he did not have the practice of using a bathing soap. Still cleaner were his heart and conscience.

He had no taste for delicious dishes. His normal food included rice, mung dal and Alu chatni (Patato Paste). His daily life included reading a chapter of Bhagawat Geeta (translated into Odia), feeding the poor and helping others. In early morning, he went out to Padma Pokhari area, which was one kilometer from his residence and come back after about half an hour to prepare for his work in the agricultural field. On return from the field at mid day, he read Bhagabat Geeta before he took his lunch. He also went to the same Padma Pokhari area in the evening, interacted with people and came back. He had a speciality, he spoke truth even under critical situations. He had a mind free from anxiety, tension, fear or threat.

He had no child- and no dream for himself or for the child. Being free from desire, he had no frustration or sense of revenge. His mind was free from anxieties generated by desires. He worked in the field and also in the market place but it was only to earn his living but not to acquire wealth. He was a fully contented person. Contentment was the shortest route to his peace and bliss. Being a Sadachari, he always stuck to truth and did not have any intention in compromising with truth. Even when his own kith and kin were involved in conflict, he always stood with truth, honesty and fair play. He was always with a smiling face even when all else in the village were upset with failure of agriculture. Some miscreants wanted to harass him in old age.

When he became very old, he left his possessions in the village and spent his last days in an Ashram in worshipping and reciting Bhajan. He loved me very much. I was very close to him and he asked me to perform certain rituals for him at Gaya after his death. By God's grace, I have fulfilled his desire.

Some of these notable elders took leadership in organizing cultural and social activities. Fixation of dates for annual Pala, the gayak (singer), venue, contributions of different families etc. were mostly done by the group consisting of young led by Fakir Muduli, Bali Swain etc. Similarly, fish catching from Padma Pokhari and distribution of fish among families were done by these two elders Fakir Muduli took charge of the Puja, Prasad, (Gaja Bhog of Kartik Purnima) in Mahadev Temple. The village had a type of court that settled disputes, among people and this work was done by Chintamni Pradhan, Kanduri Ch Swain etc.

The new face of the village

During my last visit, I decided to cover the entire village from the north to the south and have a full view of it. Normally when we come to the village, we move in about one third of the village due to lack of time and need. Besides, many of my contemporaries are either dead or are not seen active in the village. Because of the field work I did, in connection with this project, I visited almost every part of the village, its lanes and by lanes, the new houses and the new roads in the village. I became overwhelmed to see the changes and thought, what if somebody who left the village in sixties of the last century came now? Will he be able to recognize the village, its geographical and demographic features and the types of people as also their life style?

The new face of the village

Changes have been all pervading. Its earlier picture (two rows of thatched houses and between them about 12 feet kutchha passage way) is now replaced by pucca houses on both sides and the passage is a concrete road. Thatched houses are rare and are not close to the passage way. One can enter the village from East, West, North and South on a road, there is no need of entering into agricultural field, canal or small water bodies. Padma Dānda is now a very important place, it provides space for new offices. No one defecates in the open. Evenings are no more dark in the village, electricity has added to the beauty and charm of the village in darkness. Almost every house has a Television and quite a few have a V.C.P. Women no more cover their heads with the saree, they keep it open. Many of them wear salwar Punjabi or Maxi which in sixties, could not be visualized. They are no more confined to the house. They do all kinds of works earlier done by the males only. Some women of the village are working in offices. Girls of marriageable age continue their studies comfortably in the schools and colleges and parents leave the girls to themselves while going to schools, colleges or offices. Polities, which was the monopoly of the males, is now the favourite of women. They are the unavoidable part of politics. The Constitution Amendment Act has provided scope for this change.

Agriculture has undergone great changes. There is provision for plough and bullocks doing the land tilling but people prefer to use a power tiller or a tractor for better result. The village has now- tractors and power tillers which the owners give on rent for use by other people in the village. The farmers don't any more preserve paddy or dal seeds from out of their own produce, they get it from government at subsidized rates. These seeds help in greater production but, some times, inferior seeds damage the harvest and give rise to farmer unrest. Fertilizers and pesticides are an unavoidable component of farming which was not so earlier. The manure prepared out of the fire dust, the garbage as also cow dung were used by the farmers. Cow dung is now used in Gobar Gas plant. Some in the village have such plants and get electricity as also manure out of it. This was a matter of imagination in our childhood days. The farmers, these days, have become organized. There was no cure to their problems and there was no scope for them to agitate and focus their issues. Now different farmer organizations have come up. For every problem in agriculture, the farmers want government intervention and necessary remedial steps. Untimely rains, flood, cyclones, drought or even pests damage crops. These days, the government comes to the rescue of the farmers in all of their problems. Also, farmers sometime agitate for waiver of agricultural loans availed of by them in case they fail to repay the loan.

The new development which a farmer of sixties of the 20th century would not approve is the idleness noticeable in the villages of Odisha in general, and our village in particular. Quite a significant part of the cultivable land remains uncultivated- either because the land owner who earlier gave it for share cropping refuses to do so now owing to threat to his continuance as land owner or necessary labour force is not available. Part of the labour force seeks jobs in urban centres and another part of it refuses to do any labour because government provides rice at the rate of rupees one per Kg besides other allowances. Cost of labour has gone up. Some also don't cultivate more land because even without any cultivation, they are comfortable with the freebies provided by the government.

In our days, good drinking water was not available. We had to fetch water from a neighbour's well. There was a well in the midst of agricultural field. Its beauty was, when most wells in the village went dry in summer, that well only provided drinking water to many families. This well was called Bila Kua (well in the agricultural field). There was only one tube well in the entire village. Now, almost all houses have access to tube well water besides piped water supply. The village has, now, a new class of skilled labour- masons, plumbers, carpenters. Construction materials (cement, rod, metals, stone, bricks, sand etc.) are kept stored in the village.

Another thing which was unthinkable then is some Tent House. These days, celebrations of various types (marriage, sacred thread ceremony, death rites, birth day celebration, marriage Anniversary etc.) are made in the village. Therefore, this Tent House facilitates supply of utensils, carpets, chairs, lights etc. on rent. A good team of cooks has come up in the village. Some of them also come on call to Cuttack and Bhubaneswar.

Agriculture, then, was the primary concern of the people and it kept them busy regardless of whether it was profitably remunerative or not. With the application of fertilizer and other nutrients, it started being more gainful. Educational advancement in the area and more and more young me and woman with high education from village give hopes for better future. Getting jobs inside and outside Odisha and even abroad by them has led to faster economic growth of the village. Quite a few of them are in service outside India and a large number of them are in government and company services in different states of India besides many within the state of Odisha. Some, who have education and are not in any service, have started their own projects and business. New types of occupations have come up (vegetable Vender, drivers, electricians, health workers etc.).

Maa Sarala Thakurani

The Temple: Sarala temple now located at Kanakpur is not where it was originally built. The original mandir was built in the 8th century. The deity was being worshipped there till the end of Hindu rule in 1568 AD. It was at this stage that the Muslims repeatedly raided the Mandir. Repeated attacks by Sultan Suleman Karari shattered this famous Hindu shrine. It was completely destroyed during the rule of Aurangzeb. The present temple was built during the Maratha rule (1753-1803). However, who built it still remain a question. Some hold that the Raja of Manijanga built it but there is no historical evidence that Manijanga ever had a Raja. Kujang alone, in this area, had a Raja.

The sanctum sanctorum of Goddess Sarala is regarded as one of the spiritually most elevated expressions of Shaktism from time immemorial. Maa Sharala is regarded as a synthesis of the divine figures of Durga and Saraswati. The Sarala cult is an amalgamation of the principal Hindu cults (vedic, tantric and Vaishnavic).

This shrine has a legendary association with ancient sages. Sage Parshuram (believed to be an incarnation of Lord Vishnu) engraved the deity by his arrow and worshiped Her for wisdom and power. This famous Hindu temple is one of the 8 important Shakti pithas of Odisha and one of the 31 such pithas of India. Sarala is Vaishnavi and, therefore, Tulasi along with Bel leaf is used in her naivedya. As per the Skand Puran, when Sati (Parvati) immolated herself as a reaction to the disrespect shown to her husband Shiva, the latter became very angry and carried the burnt body of sati (Parvati) along with Him. Lord Vishnu became apprehensive that Lord Shiv could do anything as a result of His anger. Therefore, He sliced Sati's body into pieces which fell at different places. These pieces were 50 in number and wherever one of these pieces fell, there came up a Shaktipith. One such a piece (Parvati's tongue) fell on Jhankad (The area which included seat of Sarala temple). Maa is worshiped here in Jhankad.

The Idols: There are three idols in the sanctum sanctorum of Sarala mandir. One of these (the main idol) is an eight-armed figure (Asta bhujaa) of Goddess Sarala.

Her right foot is on the lion (Singha). She holds a khadga, a trishul, veena and Pustak in the right hands. In her left hand, she has pattisha, Karmuk, Ghanta and head of Mahishashur. She combines in Herself both Durga and Saraswati or Mahisha Mardini and Vakdevi. She is referred to as Vak Devata Sarada. The second idol is four armed (Chatrubhujaa) in the posture of giving, showering blessing (Krupa) called Varadaa i.e. granting boons. Her look and the posture add to Her magnificence. The third idol has two arms (Dwibhujaa). It is made of eight precious metals (Asta Dhatu). This is Her mobile image (Chalanti Vigraha) which goes around on special occasions.

Ma Sarala is believed to be a patron of both Vaishnavs and Shaktas. Some view her as Buddhist tantrik because she holds Veena and Ghantas (Mahayan symbols). Being Saraswati or Vakdevi, she is Goddess of wisdom and Knowledge. Adikabi Sarala Das, a great devotee of her called her in many names: Durga, Parvati, Saraswati, Vak Devi, Aparna, Mahakali, Mahalaxmi, Narayani etc. She is many in one. Her trident is Lord Shiv's, Chakra is the Sudarshan Chakra of Vishnu, bow is of Vayu, arrow is of Surya, ghanta is of Airavat and the lion is of Himavon.

Temple Festivals: Several festivals are celebrated in the Sarala Mandir but significant among them are Durga Puja (referred to earlier), Pana Sankranti, Jhamu Jatra, Chandan Jatra, Navanna Puja etc.

Chandipath during the Durga Puja was something special for me. At this phase of my life, when I recollect the scene relating to Chandi Path by the Brahmin Pandits in Sarala Mandir, quite a series of scenes come before me. I see several rows of Pandits, all well dressed with new clothes and bold sandal paste marks on their forehead seated comfortably chanting the Sapta Sati Chandi (Markandeya

Puran) in front of Ma Sarala (also called Sarada). Among these Pandits, there was an erudite Sanskrit scholar (Krupa Sindhu Pandit) who had a great fame in our area. He was coordinating the Chandipath programme. The programme started at 9AM punctually, and at 12 noon, it was over. This programme was for sixteen days (from Mulastami to Mahastami). This was the most important aspect of Durga Puja in Sarala temple. Since the temple comes on the way from our village to the school (Sarada Academy, Kanakpur) many of us had the privilege to have a darshan of Ma Sarala every day before going to the school and while returning therefrom. Ordinarily, we bowed down at the Singhadwar. On the days of Chandipath, we made it a point to reach earlier, go inside near the venue of Chandi Path (Mukhashala of the temple) and bow down before Maa Sarala and also before the pandits. We felt as if Maa Thakurani was physically present there on the spot. Sometimes, we went inside the temple premises to have Ma's Paduko (bath water) which was of very beautiful fragrance. This Paduko contained Chandan, Chua, Aguru, Madhu, Kshir, Kasturi etc. It touched Maa's sacred feet and we drank it with pleasure. Some time, we carried some of it as per the desire of our parents who utilized it in sprinkling it on the Paddy field or vegetable plants to protect them from diseases. The Paduko was also taken as a medicine for stomach problem. Mother Sarala being the best saviour in life, we believed that a darshan of Her was adequate to get necessary strength to face any situation in life.

Pana Sankranti (also called Maha Visuv Sankranti) is the first festival in a year. It occurs either on 13th or 14th April each year. This day kept us, as school going students, very active. Thousands of devotees of Sarala from different villages of the districts of Cuttack, Jagatsinghpur and

Kendrapara besides some from other districts make it a point to visit Kanakpur and have a darshan. Since they come from far off villages in the hot month of April, as per the tradition of the village, we offered Jal Chhatra (free drinking water). This Jal was called Avada Pani. Its ingredients were (a) Sri Mahaprasad (b) Curd (c) Salt and (d) Lemon Juice. We pulled water from the well of the school and supplied drinks to the thirsty pilgrims. This activity started at 8-30 am and continued up to about 6 pm. We never felt tired on this day.

Hereafter, we had a programme that made us very happy. We visited the Ma, had Her darshan, and on our way back, we enjoyed the special prasad of the day. This Prasad was Chuda Ghasa. Components of this prasad includes Chuda (Flattened rice), ghee, coconut, molasses, and a variety of spices. The Prasad becomes very tasty. About 20 to 30 families jointly organized the programme and, therefore, some members of each family took the Prasad on the way back at a place toward the end of the village Kanakpur. Whatever remained unconsumed was distributed among the participant families. The Chuda ghasa of Pana Sankranti has no parallel. I remember it on each Pana Sankranti without fail.

Another festival of 21 days programme is Chandan Jatra. It starts on the Akshaya Trutiya and the event is repeated for 21 days. On this occasion, the Chalanti Vigraha of Ma Sarala moves in a boat in the grand Tank (Called Chandan Pokhari). A whole team of Music and musical instruments and sevaks as well as purohit move in the boat. This event becomes very enjoyable- the summer evening near the source of water and the music and mantras make it very enjoyable.

Makar Sankranti is a very popular festival. It

is probably one occasion when any poor man could arrange resources to offer prasad to the Goddess. A great congregation of Bhaktas of Ma Sarala is made on this day. Every one carries some material from home to offer to Ma as a prasad. The ingredient of this prasad are sunned rice (not boiled), cheese, molases, coconut and banana.

Earlier, Durga puja was a special event. A goat was sacrificed as a part of Sandee puja. This has been discontinued. Instead of an animal, a fruit (Kusmand) is sacrificed to meet the requirement of the Puja. The beauty of Durga puja celebration lay in the Chandipath and the environment it created.

The Venerable Sanyasis of Karamala

When I recollect my past, one experience of childhood which makes me very happy is how we moved with Sadhus. As far as I remember, when I was about 8-9 years old, I came across some pious, lovable and imitable persons and sadhus. Almost every year, a small group of Sanyasis (numbering 3 to 4) visited our place in the village. They were from the Shanti Ananda Ashram of Thakur Abhiram Paramhans Dev, Karamala. I remember three of them distinctly by their name. They were Subarna Baba, Kapil Baba, and Adikand Baba. They did the favour of visiting us because my parents and our eldest brother were initiated into Thakur Abhirm's spiritual order. These sanyasis visited us and the villages nearby to provide spiritual guidance to the people besides popularizing the Abhiram Philosophy. Every time the sanyasis came, there was a new member in the group, probably, they were to be trained in how to carry the message of the Paramhans to the common people.

The group halted at a place for a maximum of three days as per the directions of their Gurudev not to cause heavy expenditure of the disciples. They also were asked to accept whatever offerings the disciple was able to give them and not to ask for special dishes. My mother prepared prasad for them. The Babas started their day's schedule after having the morning prasad (breakfast). They moved on foot from one end of our village to the other in a procession, singing and playing traditional musical instruments (Khajani, Gini, Jhanja etc.) This they called as <u>Maadhkari</u>. Such procession was also carried out in a nearby village (named Kinailo). At times, local Kirtan parties of the village accompanied them. During the procession in our village, 20 to 30 people joined the sanyasis in the Maadhkari.

Me and my brother Niranjan took this opportunity to escape from the school and join the sanyasis in the Maadhkari. The music played during the moving kirtan was enchanting. More enchanting still was the melodious singing of the Babas, particularly because the bhajans were composed by Thakur Abhiram Paramahansha. Babas sang them and all others repeated these songs. Thakur Abhiram's Koilee Bhajans were very popular. He used the Koilee as an agent to carry forward his message to the disciples as also to others who languished in spiritual darkness These Bhajans also sought to build a society remarkable from the points of view of social, cultural and spiritual attainments. Sweetness in the tone of Kapil Baba together with the contents of the Bhajan had great appeal to people's heart. For quite a while, it mesmerized the people and diverted their minds from whatsoever work they were doing.

The messages sent through the Bhajans covered a variety of problems faced by a common man, the methods of getting out of the crises and the spiritual implications of these problems and their solutions. The Bhajans were quite philosophical. I did not understand much of it though I memorized quite a lot of it. Whatever little I could understand had certainly some impact on my future course of life.

Thakur Abhiram, through the Koilee Bhajan, sent the messages to his devotees where he said, "Human life is a very rare life. It should not go waste". The human being, through actions and behaviour, can come close to the God. All actions except those undertaken in the service a God are meaningless. One need not be worried in searching for places where God inhabits because, He is present everywhere, in each grain of sand, each hill, each plant, each creature, each flower etc. One must condition his eyes to see Him in everything and everywhere. Like stars in the sky, He is present everywhere. However, ignorance (Agnan) like Surya eclipsing all the stars during day time, has made Him invisible. To see him, one has to come out of Agnan. To have the vision of the divine, one has to take the telescope of Gnan (wisdom). Gnan (wisdom) comes when the jiva adopts truthful means, renounces violence, refrains from acquiring other's wealth and women and treats all others with love, respect and cordiality like one's own.

Abhiram said that reciting mantras and repeating names of the Lord help spiritual advancement. However, a Bhakta should not limit himself to recitations only. He must practise the virtues. He has to spend time regularly in praying, remembering and meditating. Thinking of Him with fullest attention draws a bhakta close to Him. As one gets the taste of sweetness only after eating, so is the condition only when one feels intimately the presence of Him in everything.

Thakur Abhiram emphasized, therefore, on fixing uninterrupted (Aviram) attention at the Lord's Lotus feet. One must stay away from all sorts of evil thoughts because these drift the Bhakta away from the Lord. A clean and pure heart is essential for being the seat of the Lord. "Remove all dirt from your eyes, so that you will be eligible to move in right direction". Ku drusti, Ku budhi, Ku sangi and Ku das are antithetical to spiritual advancement. Do pada seva (serve his feet), the whole world is his Pada, and pada seva means serving all and loving His creations. Do all these as a part of your puja and upasana. "The Jiva has no refuge except in Paramanand (the Lord)".

During the stay of the Sanyasis in our village, Subarna Baba would address the bhaktas following the evening puja. He exhorted bhaktas to follow the message of Thakur Abhiram Paramhans. He said, those engaged in sensual pleasure are deviated from the pursuit of seeking truth and are eager for material attainments. The day for them is a dark night. Kam, Krodha, etc have made the day night for them. As a messenger of Thakur, "I urge you to wake up and see the reality and shift to the right direction." People indulge in wrong things and untruth. Thakur asked the Bhakta to adopt and uphold four ANANDS: Satya Ananda, Shanti Ananda, Daya Ananda and Kshama Ananda. Seeking for Ananda means being on the track of truth. Truthfulness becomes the first casualty of closeness to wrong tracks and evil people. Pleasure (Ananda) in truthfulness increases with a mind characterized by peace, forgiveness (Kshama) and compassion (Daya). A combination of the four Anands, as Bhagaban Abhiram said, ensures Anand everyday (Nitya). Such a person moves in right direction. He searches for pious people, desires the company of saints, reorganizes his own deficiencies (vices) and ultimately surrenders to a saint, a sadguru.

Thakur Abhiram's Bhajan seeks to arouse the Jiva to real consciousness. In another place, as Subarna Baba explained, Abhiram said those indulging in wrong things waste the valuable human life. The people whom one takes as his father, mother, wife, children etc. are not his own. His father is dharya (patience), mother's name is kshama (forgiveness), wife Shanti (peace) truth is his son and compassion is his sister. A misguided person forgets them and indulges in wrong things with wrong people. However, the God knows their problems and eagerly waits for helping them in moving on the right path.

Abhiram'S Bhajan repeatedly cautions the bhakta against Avidya and evil companion. Never give company to the evil people, whatever may be the case. Quoting from the Thakur, Subarna Baba humorously said, "Bhagawan is afraid of evil persons". The society has quite a good number of such persons. The bhakta must recognize such people and keep away from them. The lord has given us mind to distinguish between good and bad, the viveka to bring good ideas and good proposals for action. "Even then, why should you deviate from truth and move towards untruth? God has sent me to prevent you from wrong path and evil people."

Subarna Baba touched upon many issues which pollute social and cultural life. Speaking from Abhiram Koilee Bhajan, he said that an issue which tends to create tension and bitterness in the village-life was the touchable-untouchable issue. This is a nonissue and an issue that has absolutely no justification to engage people's mind. Every one including the plants and in insects having been created by Brahma, how can there can be any stratification? If at all there should be any division in the society, in must be on the basis of duties people perform as per their competence. Viewed from the gotra angle, it is amply clear that all are descendants of one Rishi or the other. All are either Rishi putra on Rishi Kanya, all are equal. However, there are some untouchables. They include those who indulge in untruth, unkindness, jealousy, greed and violence. They are condemnable people and a Bhakta must keep away from them. These evil doers should be shunned. Closeness to Ku-sanga, Ku Budhi and Ku Mati leads to Bipathi (danger).

Subarna Baba's discourses on the philosophy of Thakur Abhiram Paramhans were an unforgettable treasure. With the end of the spiritual discourse by Subarna Baba, the program came to an end. Here after, we became active and helped our mother in entertaining the revered sadhus. The prasad normally consisted of Puri, Khiri, Dalma and Khata. Some times Puri was replaced by cakes and Dalma by a mixed vegetable curry. When I remember those days, the Babas, the Koilee Bhajan as also the ideas they sought to infuse into our minds, I become emotional. I thank God that He did this kindness to me and I came across such venerable persons.

Fairs and Festivities in the Village

The village being a multi caste one, had all types of personnel to successfully organize fairs, festivals and festivities. Programmes were drawn by some village elders backed by young men. Participation of all the villagers was always assured, each household contributed in cash, kind or both for success of the programme. One such program was the Annual Paalaa.

Three teams, each led by one principal singer (Gayak) were very famous then. They were Hari Nath, Niranjan Kar and Baishnab Pradhan. Our village unfailingly invited one or two of these singers each year during the month of April-May. Each team presented a program for about three hours. The program started at about 7 PM and ended 6 to 7 hours later.

Since these singers were the most famous in the area, beside our villagers, those from nearby villages also came to observe the program. These programs were highly educative for the village community. Such programme exposed them to the scriptures, the literature of eminent Odia and Sanskrit poets and the essential values of our culture. I remember, we were then in primary/ Middle English schools and were much benefited by seeing the programs.

Kartik Purnima in Ishaneshwar Mahadev Mandir: Villagers worshipped Lord Ishaneshwar Mahadev and offered prasad on various occasions. Once in a year, a special program was organized in the temple on the occasion of Kartik Purnima (Full Moon day in the month of Kartik) Families contributed as per their ability and were given *Gaja Bhog* (as it was called) consisting of cake, khiri and curry. I must say that I can never forget taste of this Prasad. Fakir Muduli managed this programme each year.

Individually some people do some special puja and seek the grace of Lord Ishaneswar. Almost every month, there was some such puja in the temple. Some of these programmes end with a Baal Bhog (Feed the Children). The devotees normally wait for the school time – at the close of the school hours, they invite the students at the school gate (all were small children reading in the Primary School) for the Bhoji. I remember, all of us were very happy to accept the invitation. Instead of going home, we almost rushed to the temple for the prasad. The prasad consisted of very ordinary items but it tasted very nice. The Prasad included rice, dalma and khiri but its taste was unforgettable. I don't know if such programmes are still there and whether children take prasad with as much pleasure as we did.

Ishaneshwar mahadev temple

Rajo and the Bagudi Khel: This is a joyful celebration of the 3-day Annual Rajo festival (Which comes on 13th June to 15th June or 14th June to 16th June). Since the farmers normally complete sowing of paddy seeds by this time, this is an occasion for the village community to enjoy and make merry.

The Annual Rajo was celebrated with great pomp and grandeur in the villages. Cakes of various types were prepared in each house. A special type of cake, known as Pod Pitha (burnt cake), prepared on this occasion was very famous. Even these days, people say rajo without Pod Pitha is a sad experience. However, there is a difference now. Earlier house wives prepared it at home, now people purchase it from shops, hotels or some other agencies. There are many shops in Cuttack and Bhubaneswar where the pod pitha is sold and people purchase it from there. We had a good number of cocoanut trees and my mother made adequate use of this cocoanut, molasses rice and Biri (black gram) in preparing the pod pitha. Those who did not have cocoanut, they prepared it without it. Both the varieties of cakes were tasty. Another important food item was mutton curry. Almost all families had it during the Rajo. Out of the three days of Rajo, the second day is a Sankranti day when non vegetarian food was almost prohibited. Families could have mutton curry on the first and or third days. Not having it was a sad experience. Most people in the village had mutton curry only once in a year during the Rajo.

School-going children get new dress, women, particularly the newly married ones, have new sarees on the occasion. I remember how we got prepared for Rajo celebration. Turmeric paste was applied to our bodies before bath. We took pod pitha, wore new dresses, had varieties of spices like labang, Gujarati, Elachi etc for our consumption. We then moved with friends till lunch time and, after lunch, we went to the field to view Bagudi now known as Kabaddi.

Dolapurnima: Dolapurnima, the full-moon day of the month of Phalgun (March) is an auspicious day for the Hindus who worship Lord Krishna and His consort Radha. The metal idols of Radha and Krishna, kept in the village temple, were cleaned, new clothes were put on them and the idols were carried in a procession by about eight persons in a palanguin to a place where similar idols from other villages assembled. After some worshiping rituals, people applied phagu (Fragrant Power of different colours) on the idols and also on each other. They sing <u>Bhajans</u> and make merry. This is done at night and therefore, in the then villages of Odisha where there was no electricity, Petro-Max lights were carried by each team, thus, the meeting place (melan) was profusely lighted. The atmosphere became exuberant and convivial.

Not only do the idols meet in Melan, several other categories of people also get an opportunity to meet and make merry. Temporary shops and stalls selling sweets, other tasty food, articles of house hold needs, children's toys and balloons are opened on that day. Both the categories of people, the sellers and purchasers, make the Melan highly enjoyable. They shower of <u>Avir</u>/ <u>Phagu</u> on each other after doing so on the idols. This begins what is known as HOLI or HORI. It is believed to have been played by Bhagaban Krishna with maids including Radha of <u>Gopa</u> (the Kingdom of Krishna). In recent years, there seems to be some change. People play Holi quite actively and passionately. They take the Melan as an occasion of merrymaking. The Radhakrishna Melan is held every year.

I remember how I attended the Melan along with a few others from the village. The venue of the Melan was about 3 kms from our village and we walked up the whole distance, The lights, the congregation and the shops as also the food items we got from the shop made us very happy. We came back late in the night. Because it was a full-moon night, there was no need of light on the way back home. These days, the lovers of Melan find the journey pleasant because of the pucca road, suitable for mother cycles/ scooters or even cars.

Chapter-II

Me, My Family and Friends

My grandfather (Keshari Nanda) and his elder brother Banchhanidhi were the two sons of Dharmu Nanda. Dharmu did not have much of a landed property. The elder son Banchhanidhi was well read on the Karma Kanda and the scriptures. Banchhanidi was a tall and handsome person and Keshari, his younger brother was quite different. Unlike the elder brother, he was unmindful in learning and had the ambition to be rich for which he left home to try his luck at Calcutta. He also earned a lot of money and, each time he came to village, he purchased some land.

Like Banchhanidhi, his wife Hari was quite simple, affectionate and pious. Banchhanidhi was a devotee of lord shiva (Ishaneshwar Mahadev) and each day he took food only after performing his daily rituals at the Shiva temple. His wife Hari too observed several bratas and fasts. Keshari's wife (Sati) came from a big land owners' family. Unfortunately for Keshari, Sati died when Bhagabat, her only child (my father) was only five-year-old. The little Bhagabat was taken care of by his Badabou (Banchhanidhi's wife) and he was brought up well. Hereafter, he was taken

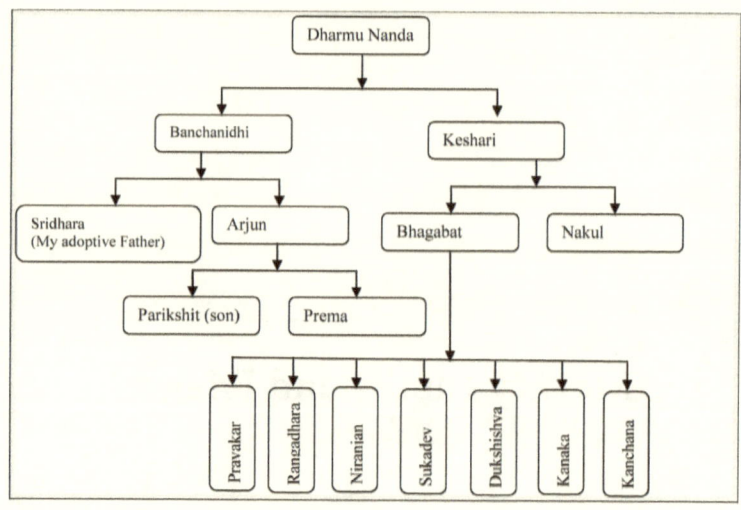

by his maternal grandfather and was kept for some time. On return, to the village, he was given a good training in Sanskrit and various mantras and Puja procedures by Banchhanidhi. Since my father had a sweet tone, he could sing very nicely. His pronunciation of Sanskrit Slokas was clean and flawless. That made him famous in the locality. He also had good education in Sanskrit.

Banchhanidhi had eight daughters and two sons (Sridhar and Arjun). Both of the sons were younger than Bhagabat. All of them were very close to each other. Banchhanidhi however, carried Bhagabat on his shoulder while asking both Sridhar and Arjun to walk in case the children accompanied him to any place. Sridhar (My adoptive father whom I called as Ba) told me how Bhagabat was the apple of Banchhanidhi's eyes.

Banchhanidhi got Keshari remarried and a step mother in Labanya (Naban) for Bhagabat came to the family. She bore a son (Nakul) and a daughter for Keshari. Keshari continued trying his luck at Calcutta and went on adding to family property. Banchhanidhi did not live long.

The marriages of the sons (Bhagabat and Sridhar) were solemnized. Bhagabat had to marry Chakradhar Dash's daughter (Gehlarani) as per the oral commitment of his late mother (Sati) and mother of Gehlarani in early childhood days. Compared to Keshari Nanda, Chakradhar Dash was more eminent in the locality and had more landed property. The new relations added to Keshari's standing in the village and in the locality. We, five brothers and two sisters were born to Bhagabat and Gehlarani. Eldest brother whom we all brothers called Bhaina, was Pravakar. Second to him was Rangadhar. The third brother was Niranjan, myself the fourth and the youngest was Dukhishyam. The two sisters Kanak and Kanchan were younger than all the brothers. Keshari separated Sridhara and Arjun after getting them married. He, however, gave them equal share of the property.

Bhaina had his education in Kanakpur, Korua High School and Christ College, Cuttack. He was the first graduate of our village and of the locality spreading over a radius of five-kilometers. He was an eye opener for many and was the first gazetted officer (O.F.S) of the village. He also displayed qualities of goodness and love for those who needed it badly.

Keshari's younger son (my father's step brother) was of the same age as of my Bhaina. His marriage was held simultaneously with Bhaina's marriage. Immediately after this marriage, my father was separated by his step mother. We the five brothers, two sisters and parents constituted a big family and to that extent, the property given to our father was quite inadequate. My father had no complaint and he silently accepted whatever was given to him. It was at this stage that our maternal grandparents came to his rescue. Bapa's cousin Arjun had some job at Calcutta and

Sridhar managed agriculture and did the Puja etc. in the village and they were economically quite comfortable. Ba loved and respected Bapa very much and he came to his help in this period of crisis.

Bhaina & Nuabou

Our eldest brother (Pravakar) is addressed as Bhaina and his wife (Our Bhauja is called Nuabou) had been a very powerful factor in our lives. In fact, Bhaina being the first person in the locality to become a graduate and to become the first gazetted offier, in the locality, he was much liked and respected. He became a model for the village youth and parents in the village gave his example to their growing sons. The term 'Nuabou' is a typical Odia term which means 'new Mother'. The position and status of a Nuabou is more or less like that of a mother, she is expected to be so in relation to her Dewars (younger brothers of her husband) and Nanand (sisters of her husband). Our Nuabou joined our family when I was quite young, a lower primary school going lad. Myself and my other brothers were glad to a have Nuabou, a new person with whom we could talk, play, quarrel etc. She was a very calm and quiet person. I remember that I gave her a lot of problems in those days. My elder brother (Nirabhai) was still worse in giving problems to her. She would face all these, solve them and still not complain. Her husband was the primary earning member of the family and, normally in such case, she could have claimed a special status and special consideration in all matters. She had none of these. She always gave first preference to the welfare of all, care of our parents, education and health of youngsters. She had very limited needs. Bhaina also had similar attitude. Both seemed made for each other. In so doing, Bhaina probably neglected his own children. His children, particularly his daughter (Nalini), eldest son (Abhiram) and youngest son (Shantaram) were good students and had he taken due care of their education, they could have been better placed in their lives. My mother expired in 1982 when she was 67-year-old. Bapa lived up to his 100th year (2005) only because of the loving care taken by Nuabou. Both for Bapa ad Bou, Nuabou was the dearest. She was the source of all comfort, happiness and confidence. Nuabou expired in 2020 at the age of 88 years. It was an irreparable loss for the family.

My father with my Bhaina,
his son Abhiram and grandson Gopal (Four generation)

Bā's Family

My Bā's younger brother (Sanbapa), named Arjun was very close to him. He, his wife Padma (San Bou) and her two children (daughter Prema and Son Parikshit) as also me and Bā constituted a separate family. I was adopted to this family when I was two-year-old. Prema was four years younger than me. Parikshit was born much later when I was about 16-year-old. San Bapa and San Bou did not have much of a change in their attitude towards me after the birth of Parikshit. Prema was married in 1962 to a Sanskrit Pandit but unfortunately, she did not have a stable conjugal life. May be, it was because she could not manage well. She stayed in our place almost permanently. After I joined as a Lecture in Berhampur University, my wife along with San Bapa, San Bou and Parikshit stayed with me at Berhampur and Parikshit had his education in the school.

How Bā adopted me

When I was about two and a half years old, my Bā lost his wife (Navi) who delivered a girl child. The child expired immediately after the death of the mother. Therefore, Bā was depressed. I was the only tool to change his mind. As such, he loved me and played with me and after the sad demise of his wife and daughter in quick succession, he took me closest to his heart. Wherever he went, he never forgot me. He gave me some gift or other when he came back. I also loved him much, and whenever he came back home, I presented before him a long list of grievances against others including my father and mother. Despite every one's motivation, Bā firmly decided not to remarry. In the meantime, he in his heart, had decided to adopt me as his son. My parents did not agree. Bā, therefore, approached some elders whom my parents held in esteem. They urged upon my father and mother to allow me on adoption to Bā. After a lot of persuasion even by my maternal grandfather, Bapa agreed and Bā succeeded. I became his son since then. My being adopted did not make much difference in the beginning. I remained as I was, but at night, I slept near Bā rather than near my mother. In course of time, I took my breakfast, lunch and dinner with Bā in his house and, occasionally, when some special dishes were prepared in my parents' house, I also took it there. A feeling gradually developed in me that I belong to Bā's house rather than that of my parents.

I was admitted to the school as my Bā's son and, as a result, officially I became his son. My Bā was happy that I stood first in class in the schools, won scholarships and had a high First Division in the H.S.C Exam. He had a sense of vanity that his son alone, in that locality, had a First Division with high percentage of marks in the HSC examination. Bā was a highly affectionate person and cared a little for his self. He loved my father and took pride in saying that he happened to be his brother. He was equally affectionate to his younger brother, Arjun, my San Bapa (Uncle). San Bapa worked in a factory in Calcutta and he supported my education up to a level when Biju Patnaik began helping me in 1961 (September).

An unintended Shock

As a good student, I had my own plan of a career and therefore, I concentrated on my studies. Bā had a different plan, he wanted me to get married. An undesirable person of the village motivated him to actively go ahead with it. One evening, just before the commencement of my first-year degree examination, Bā arrived in the Hostel of Revenshaw College to consult me with regard to my marriage with a particular girl. I explained to him that I was not prepared for the marriage at that age and in that phase of my educational career. Bā insisted. He threatened that he would not be back to the village if I did not agree. To avoid the tension during examination time, I gave my unwilling consent and after he left, I wrote a letter to the girl's father that in case he went ahead with the proposal, I would take the help of police since his daughter was below 18 years of age. The proposal failed and Bā had a severe jolt. He was shocked and I also felt ashamed. After about six months, our relation became normal and Bā expressed that he should not have thought of my marriage so soon. After 3 years, he again thought of my marriage. This time, he recruited support of Bapa and Bhaina and almost made my escape difficult. My marriage was solemnized on 9 May, 1966. Bā became very happy. He was affectionate, kind and forgiving.

My Marriage

Bā felt restless about my marriage. For him, once the son has become a graduate, he can easily get a job to manage himself and the family. Type, nature and social estimate of the job were not part of his consideration. When I passed the BA (Hons) examination and was in MA. Part I Class, he thought that it was already late for him to put me in wed-lock. He almost finalized one of the proposals in a family located at a distance of about 10 km. This time, he did not consult me, nor did he give any indication to my father but he disclosed it in course of discussion with Bhaina who had come to the village. He had all the praise for the girl, her parents, their house etc. He even urged upon Bhaina to visit the girl's family to verify if the choice was right. This gave Bhaina an opportunity to play some role in the decision on my marriage. He visited the village. On his returns, Bhaina was careful in regard to his opinion. He praised the girl, her parents and the excellent hospitality given to him. Then Bā started pointing out a dark side of the proposal which Bhaina also dittoed. Bā, hereafter, did not take even a minute to declare that he would never bring a daughter-in-law from that family.

In the meantime, a proposal came to Bhaina from a family which was very well known to us. Bhaina advised them to contact Bā directly. Bā visited that village and expressed his approval and associated Bapa also with it. The girl belonged to my maternal aunts' family and therefore, members of both sides knew each other. The marriage was finalized and I knew nothing about it. I had accompanied Bhaina to Karamala Ashram of Abhiram Paramhansha Dev, Bhaina's spiritual gurudev. When we returned therefrom to the residence of Bhaina at Bhubaneswar, I saw Bapa waiting for us. Bapa asked me to accompany him to the village next morning. He did not tell me anything about the marriage though I surmised that it could be something relating to marriage. I had no idea that it was finalized. Bapa was grave, Bhaina was silent and Nuabou, like herself, was mute.

Within an hour of our reaching the village, my would-be father-in-law and his brothers as also a few relatives, reached our place with *Tulasi* garland and prasad from Goddess *Sarala*. Bapa asked me to touch the feet of the father-in-law and other respectable persons. Unknowingly, I was made to commit and the marriage was fixed even though I had not seen the girl, nor did I know her name.

Me and my wife

I felt helpless. I was yet to complete my MA, get the job of my choice, get myself well established and be at least equal to my peers, if not superior. Sky seemed to fall down on me. I was also one of those who ridiculed people who married during their studentship. I felt that I had fallen in the estimate of my contemporaries. Another thing that agitated me was my elder brother (Niranjan) was yet to marry and I was superseding him. It did not sound well of me. The news of my marriage being fixed was known to all in no time.

My marriage was solemnized on 9th Mar, 1966 in their village 'San Adhanga'. The distance between my village and that of my father-in-law was about 10 Kilometers but one had to cross the Taladanda Canal and three rivers (Mahanadi, Paika and Chitrotpala) to reach there. There was no road connection between the two villages. The only mode of transport was bullock cart. I was, however, carried in a *Palanquin* and the newly married wife came in a Sabari. The Barat Party either went in bullock cart or cycles. Crossing the sand filled river beds of the rivers in the hot month of May was the experience that I can never forget.

My In Law's Family

My father-in-law, Prafulla Kumar Mishra was the son of Hari Charan Mishra (1866-1942) of village San Adhanga. Hari Charan Mishra had limited formal education but he was known as an erudite scholar. He was said to be conversant with fourteen Indian and Foreign languages. He had a very well-built library which gave evidence of his scholarship. He had obtained a large collection of books by post. Most of the books, after being read, were put in the packet that brought them from Britain by the Postal Department. He attached a hand written note to each book, giving, therein, his comments on the book. I had the privilege to see part of his library in some almirahs in seventies. I was amazed to see some of the most famous books of polities in his library and I brought a few of them for me. I have got some of them xeroxed and bound again. His interests included Philosophy, Religion, Astronomy, Palmistry, Politics etc. However, he was known for his knowledge in Philosophy. As is learnt, he taught Philosophy in Ravenshaw College for some time. He was, for sometime, the Dewan of Bamanda (now in Sambalpur district) and Member, Jury at Kendrapara. Various stories were heard in our childhood days about his peculiar ways of behaviour.

My father-in-law had five brothers, he being the youngest. His eldest brother Gopabandhu Mishra married the sister of my mother and, thus was my Mausha (uncle). Next to him was Lokanath Mishra who, after his education (MA in English), joined the freedom movement and congress politics. He was elected as MLA for three terms and also he became the Deputy Speaker of the Odisha Legislative Assemby.

Lokanath Mishra's brothers (except the eldest and youngest) became part of the freedom movement and activities.

My father-in-law was a Science teacher in the Korua High School. He had two daughters and five sons. My wife was his eldest child. Two of her brothers occupied important positions, one Pradipta is now a General Manager in the ONGC and the other one Prasanta was a high-ranking Bank Officer. Her younger sister (Anu) was an Associate Professor in Political Science and she retired as a Degree College Principal. Her husband, Ramakant Mishra was also an Associate Professor of English. Ramakant is more known as a dramatist, actor and poet.

My father in law

My Children

I was blessed with three daughters (Arati, Shashwati and Shrabanti) and a son (Suman). Arati was born on 12th June, 1968. The 12th June being my date of birth, her birth on the same day was said to be a good luck for me. She was named by my mother. She named her as Arati because she herself was in Artta (helpless state of mind) owing to the alarming health condition of my wife at the time of delivery. Arati was quite healthy at birth and she had a bunch of beautiful hair on her head. My second daughter Shashwati was born on 22 Nov, 1970 and the third daughter Shrabanti was born on 21, Sept, 1972. The only Son Suman was born on 27th Nov, 1974. Whereas Arati and Suman were born in the Capital Hospital at Bhubaneswar, Shashwati and Shrabanti were born in the Berhampur Medical College Hospital. The family had nick names for all my children. Arati is called Kulu, Shashwati is called Bhulu and Shrabanti's nick named as Milu. Suman was called Bapu. Arati and Shashwati started their primary education in the campus school at Bhanja Bihar (Berhampur university Campus). They joined the school at Jyotivihar (Sambalpur University Campus) when I shifted to Sambalpur University. Shrabanti and Suman started their education in Jyotivihar Campus only. All of them gave evidence of being good students right from the beginning. Arati joined the BA (Hons) course in Politicall Science after completing her Intermediate course in science. She stood first in both the Honours and Postgraduate examinations and won three Gold Medals. She also qualified in the NET conducted by the UGC. She could not try her luck in Academics only because my son-in-law serving in ONGC was posted at distant places like Gujarat, Mumbai and Assam. She therefore joined in the Life Insurance Corporation. Shashwati had her career in Economics both at the Honours and Masters levels. Having a Master's degree in First Class, she switched over to Cost Accountancy. Shrabanti had a first-class Honours in Zoology and thereafter, she switched over to Business Management. She had a very bright career but she chose to work in industry. She is now the Deputy General Manager in the Johnson Hitachi company at Delhi.

Biswamohan and Arati

Suman was a brilliant student and had a uniformly brilliant career. He qualified for admission in the I.I.T., Kharagpur but I chose to put him in the University College of Engineering, Burla in the B.E. (Electronics) because of the apprehensions caused by the atrocities committed in ragging in the I.I.T in the few preceding years. He worked in several reputed companies (Infosys, Wipro, L&T etc.) and within a period of about ten years, he rose to the position of leadership in the Company. He was in-charge of the company's business in European countries along with South Africa. He was posted at London. Prior to that, he worked in Australia and United States. He was a tee to taller and vegetarian. He left us abruptly forever and we could not know the cause of his death. God alone knows what caused his death and He alone will give justice to Suman.

Amulya and Shashwati

Sunil and Shrabanti

My eldest Son-in-law (Biswamohan) belongs to an illustrious Zamindar family of Pankapal, a village hardly 15 kilometers from my own village. He was a brilliant student of Chemistry. After his Masters in Chemistry, he joined ONGC. He is a General Manager, of Oil and Natural Gas Corporation(ONGC), a Govt. of India undertaking, currently posted at Bhubaneswar. My second son-in-law (Amulya Ratna) is the son of an Engineer and his native village in the district of Dhenkanal. He is now working as National Manager in the Reliance Insurance Company at Bombay. My third son-in Law (Sunil) is from the state of Kerala. He is serving in the Oxford University Press, New Delhi. All three are very sociable and caring.

The House at Niladri Vihar

Search for a Piece of Land: I did not inherit any landed property from my adoptive father who donated all that he had to his younger brother's son (Parikshit). Nor did I claim any property from my father when he distributed it among my other four brothers. I was, in fact, landless although my wife had some property given to her by her father. Getting a piece of land to build a house to stay after retirement became a major problem for me. Land at Bhubaneswar was costly and I lost all hopes to get it. I had applied to the government for it once but I did not get it. I planned to purchase some land at Sambalpur (near university Campus) and almost finalized for a piece of land. Before I made the agreement, I consulted some of my friends. One of them, (Prof. B Patel), a colleague of mine in the Department visited the place and appreciated the location and the price of the plot. However, he said that my purchasing that plot and settling there after retirement would not be wise. He gave good justification for his views. Since I belonged to the coastal Odisha, all my relations belonged to the places near Cuttack and Bhubaneswar. These places were more developed areas in the state, I should settle down there to avoid the problem of helpnessness and loneliness in old age, Patel opined. Jyoti Vihar would be without any delight when friend and colleagues retire from service and go back to their own places. Not many students would find it possible to visit me and take any care of me. On the other hand, since all my brothers, those of my wife and my sister-in-law had already settled at Bhubaneswar, they would quite often visit me and save me from loneliness and helplessness in old age, I dropped the idea of settling at Sambalpur.

Once during my visit to Bhubaneswar, my nephew (eldest brother's son-Abhiram) brought an application form and asked me to sign on it for a government plot to be available on lottery. I told him that I had frustrating experience in the past and it would add to the number of failures only. However, he managed to complete the formalities after obtaining my signature to submit the application. Later, I realized that had I not accepted the advice of Abhiram, I would not have got a plot of land at Bhubaneswar. I forgot about it hereafter. It was after about 2 years that my eldest brother (Bhaina) informed me that I had been allotted a plot as a result of the lottery made by the government and I should arrange about Rs.50,000/- for payment toward price of the land. I got the land on lease and it was registered in my name in 1988. As per the Lease Agreement, the proposed residential house should be constructed within 5 years. I had no money to undertake the construction work. However, I started taking steps for construction only because the university advanced a house building loan of Rs.80,000/- in my favour. Construction of the ground floor started in November, 1994 and it was completed in March, 1997.

Construction of House: The first floor was completed in 2003 when I retired from Sambalpur University. Thus, I had a permanent address which until then was the quarters of the university (B-6) occupied by me. My daughter Arati, on hearing about the house being ready for occupation told me, over phone from Shiv Sagar, "We have now our own house. This speaks of the frustration that lay in the minds of my children owing to their lack of an own house."

Construction of the house at Niladri Vihar, Bhubaneswar was a challenge from several points of view. I did not have much money at my disposal. Staying at Sambalpur, I had none of my own on whom I could depend and entrust the business to supervise/ monitor construction work. My brother's house at Pallaspalli, where I could stay if I came to supervise the work, was at a distance of 15 kms. Lack of a vehicle made this problem really difficult. There were some other relations but I could not take advantage of their stay in the vicinity of Niladri Vihar. Fortunately, the son-in-law (Dillip) and daughter (Lily) of a very close friend (I treat him as my elder brother), who stayed nearby, heard about my problem and came to offer their help. Their help was not only great but timely too which I can never forget. Dillip almost made a habit to visit the work site before he went to his office and on his return therefrom. The progress in work was communicated to me over telephone almost every day. In fact, he even offered financial help which I could return at my convenience. I am afraid, had he not intervened in the process, the cost of construction would have increased without any material differences. Quite possibly, the builder would have grabbed the house. I came to learn about this builder's background later. He had forcefully occupied some houses which he built at somebody else's land and cost. He carried a pistol. Dillip guarded against him and asked me to carefully relieve him without any unpleasantness. I accepted his advice and when I relieved the builder, he made imaginary demand of arrears and I paid for them without any question.

My son (Suman) was a student in the University College of Engineering at Burla and was not in a position to help in any way. He did his best when he joined the Infosys company at Bhubaneswar in 1999. My eldest son-in-law (Biswamohan) helped me in various ways in connection with construction of the house.

Then came the real Problem: Construction work was more or less within my control as long as it did not relate to the government. The builder built the house and money was paid by me. But the problem started when there was question of water and electricity connection. Niladri Vihar, at that time, was hopelessly desolate except for one house in the northern side of my house and another in my row. Even the one house which stood in my row was without water and electricity supply. The houses situated in the northern side of my house were built and sold by the Bhubaneswar Development Authority (BDA) which ensured water and electricity supply.

My plot was in the first row, behind the BDA colony. All plots in the southern side of the BDA houses were under the control of the General Administration (G.A.) Department of the government. Although roads were laid, water supply was not available. This prevented people from starting construction. Lack of habitation in Niladri Vihar encouraged antisocial elements to create every possible mischief. Once I saw a robust young man stealing pipes etc. which were meant for water supply. I asked him not to do so as this was necessary for water supply to this area. His reply was straight forward, "since many others are doing so, why I should not?" However, he promised me not to repeat this act. A few days later when I saw him repeating his action, I tried to prevent him but this was not possible since he was much younger and I being an old Professor, was no match for his strength and stamina. However, I gathered some courage to chase him for about half a kilometer before I abandoned the adventure.

I approached all possible government officers of the Public Health Department, each one (The Junior Engineer, Asst. Engineer, Executive Engineer) promised to provide water supply in about a month. Relying on them for one month each, I felt helpless. All that I was told by others was that some speed money need be paid. I felt humiliated to offer any speed money and I also did not know how to do it. I continued my efforts for water supply without payment of under the table amount. Ultimately, I met the Chief Engineer through a friend of mine. He promised to do it in a month. When I approached him after completion of one month period, he said it would not be possible since the Department was not ready for it. It seemed too much for me. I decided to approach my friend cum relatives who was an Additional Chief Secretary to see if he could help me in this matter. He reprimanded the Chief Engineer for the way the Department had ill-treated me and he himself was so negligent in the matter. His last sentence over telephone to the Chief Engineer was, "You must ensure water supply within twenty-four hours." He then, asked me to approach none else. When I reached my residence after about 45 minutes, I saw 2 government Jeeps of P.H.E.D. (of the Junior Engineer and the other of the S.D.O.) standing in front of my house. I was promised that water supply to my house would be provided the next day. In less than 24 hours, I was able to get water supplied by the Public Health

Engineering Department (PHED). This incident speaks of the mind set of some of the government officials. They harass the common men till they are forced to pay bribe to avoid physical and mental harassment as also unnecessary repetition of wasteful expenditure incurred in frequent visit to the government office. It is only when the common man is able to counter harass them, they start doing their work. Had I not got such a highly placed friend of mine, my suffering would have continued for long.

With regard to electricity and telephone connection, I had lesser hardship. Initially, I was provided electricity connection at commercial rate. It continued for about a year until an officer of that Department offered to help me in sorting out the problem. As regards telephone, the son-in-law of an old student who was an officer in the Telephone Bhawan made it possible for me to get it. In a way, Niladri Vihar, the phase to which I belong, became fit for habitation owing to the hard work undertaken by me. Efforts by those who came later have developed the place as a good residential colony. I remember a relation who was trying to purchase some land to build a house, was shown a plot near my house. He reacted saying "this is totally unfit for habitation. It would continue to be so at least for 20 years." He regretted his comments and decision a few years later. Niladri Vihar is now one of the best residential areas with all facilities.

Suman's Marriage

My son's marriage seemed to be a real problem for me. The various proposals which came for consideration were rejected by him though some of them were very good and from the families of cultural background similar to that of ours. I gave full responsibility to Suman to choose his life partner but he did not show much interest in that. My apprehension was that he would be sent again to US by the company and once he went, he would stay there for at least two to three years or more and like earlier occasions, his marriage would be delayed. Coming from a middle-class family, and having given my daughters in marriage without dowry, I was determined not to accept any dowry. So also, was the attitude of Suman whose options included that the girl should be an engineer and smart enough to manage things in far off lands. No dowry would be accepted. It was at this stage that the proposal for his marriage came for the daughter of a lady whose husband (Chandrasekhar Panda) had died about 5 years back and her daughter (Dipti) was an Electrical Engineering from K.I.I.T of Bhubaneswar. The girl was good to look at and my son approved the proposal. We also agreed to solemnize the marriage, particularly in view of the imminent programme of Suman going to US any time thereafter.

Chandrasekhar Panda was an employee in the defense establishment at Charbatia (Choudwar) and when he died, his wife had to depend on the family pension received from the government and the limited landed property which the family had in the village besides the family's small savings. The poor widow Manorama had two daughters and a son, the elder daughter Dipti being in the K.I.I.T doing her engineering course and the son and the other daughter were in School. Manorama could manage during this difficult time owing to the help extended by one of her brothers. The family stayed in a house constructed by Chandrasekhar at Choudwar. Chandrasekhar had a brother who (as was told by Dipti) was indifferent to the problems of the distressed family. Chandrasekhar's mother who was a mental patient stayed with her daughter. Dipti, after completing her engineering course was engaged in the ICICI Bank at Cuttack. Taking the background of the family, my elder brother and father would not have agreed to the proposal. My father particularly would not have liked the idea of bringing a daughter in law from such a family. However, none of these considerations and factors had any impact on our decision. The date of marriage was fixed, engagement held and we distributed invitation cards. Hardly three days before the scheduled day for marriage, a former student of mine who was a senior officer of the L.I.C visited our family with his wife and gave details against the girl's background and that of her mother. I was shocked. I had already posted invitation cards to friends living in far off places and distributed cards to nearby friend and relatives. By this time, I had already raised my hands before Lord Jagannath, promising to marry my son to this particular girl in the engagement function. I enquired about this from the girl's mother who dismissed all these as false. Somehow, I felt that she was right. This seemed so to me particularly owing to the girl's helplessness caused by her father's death. Also, I knew, in some situations, mischief mongers harassed girls from weaker background in spreading baseless stories against them. My son did not give any importance to the scandal. The marriage was solemnized, though with a change of venue. It was held at a good Hotel in Bhubaneswar and owing to the financial background of the girl's mother, major part of the expenses was borne by us.

Suman after Marriage: Within a month of the marriage, I realized that I had not married my son to a right girl but I had no control thereafter over the situation. Myself and my wife, suffered silently without giving any idea of it to Suman. Suman left for US with Dipti and was there for about 2 years when he came back, he told us something about his experience with the behaviour of Dipti. We advised him to adjust with her. While in U.K. in 2005, he left Infosys joined Wipro, T.C.S. and L&T in quick successions.

L&T gave him high position and fabulous pay package. In that capacity, he was in charge of the company activities in 14 countries including South Africa. The immediate casualty was his health. Dipti joined a Bank and came in contact with different people. She developed a network of friendship.

Suman had a different background. He knew good cooking, preparing cakes and sweets and he derived pleasure in entertaining friends with his vegetarian food. He loved good food and did not hesitate to spend for it. Things changed after his marriage when some one else put her control over Suman's purse. We, me and my wife, visited them in May, 2008 and stayed there for some time. We were shocked to see the type of food he took and the life he lived. His breakfast, most of the time, consisted of an apple. His day began early in the morning and he came back home after about ten hours. On most days, he was on tour. There was no certainty of the nature, quality and quantity of his food. On the days he was at home in the evening, we found him cooking the food for all. Dipti was totally indifferent to domestic work which Suman was doing. As we understood, Suman deliberately did everything by himself to avoid unpleasantness.

Dipti had several strategies to isolate Suman from all others. Even though she tried to start with me, she realized that it was too difficult, almost impossible. Her next target was my eldest daughter Arati whom Suman loved and respected because, as he often said, she was more intelligent than him. Dipti tried to poison Suman's ears. Arati tried to avoid any crisis, gradually keeping away from Suman, in avoiding talking for long with him over telephone. Even when both of them came to India, unlike on earlier occasions when most of the times they were invited to lunch/dinner at Arati's place, the frequency was reduced. Shashwati was at Bangalore or Mumbai and, therefore, when they came to India, they had no chance of meeting her and her family unless they decided to visit her. She being an introvert, silent and Philosophical in approach did not probably provoke much anger in Dipti. Shrabanti, my youngest daughter, though older than Suman, always held him as her real guardian. Suman's views and opinions were final for her even. In her estimate, all others were less well informed. Dipti tried to misbehave with her in showing off her own affluence and foreign outlook. She tried to do so in offering some electronic gadgets which Shrabanti continuously turned down. Shrabanti became apprehensive that Dipti would cause trouble in her relation with Suman. Suman, however, maintained due relations with his sisters and reprimanded them for their shrinking behaviour.

Bratopanayan of Anwesh

My grandson (Arati's Son) Anwesh had his upanayan on 17th Jan, 2007. Suman loved Anwesh very much and had high hopes from him. He motivated him for higher education in first rate educational institutions outside India and offered to finance him. About 4 month's earlier, Biswamohan, my eldest Son-in-law, informed Suman over telephone about the upanayana. In this typical Brahmin function, the presence of the maternal uncle was essential since he does a good lot of <u>Karm</u> on this occasion. We were apprehensive that Dipti would create some problem to prevent Suman's coming to Bhubaneswar.

However, Suman, on hearing from Biswamohan, said that he would reach much before the date and enjoy his nephew's Upanayan Karm. He came along with Dipti and became a part of the celebrations. These days when he has left us forever, we sometimes see the video recording of the Upanayan and console ourselves.

Tiara, my grand-daughter (Shashwati's daughter) was Suman's great favourite. It was Suman who (then) from Australia, named her as Tiara, the whitest bird. Even though her official name is Ashavaree, she is known as Tiara in the family circles. Suman would always send dress which matched her colour. He would also send toys for her. In his last visit to India on 1, May, 2009, he came to India via Mumbai and spent a day with Tiara and Shaswati. That was the last they saw him and received his love. Suman's untimely demise caused much problem for Shaswati and she is still not fully free from it.

I Visited London

My son (Suman) and daughter-in-Law (Dipti) stayed at London. Suman was a senior executive in L&T in change of business of the company in all European countries besides that in South Africa. Dipti had a job in a bank. Nature of Suman's job made him undertake frequent tours for nearly three days in a week. Dipti working in a nearby bank had a leisurely life.

Suman had several times asked me and his mother to visit him in United States where he worked for some years. It was not possible for us to do so. During his stay at London, he asked us to come but I avoided any trip outside India owing to my preoccupation with the all-round development of Fakir Mohan University. When my day of retirement from FM University came closer, he made all arrangements for the trip and fixed date for it. As such, both of us left for London in May, 2008. In the preceding evening, we reached our daughter Shrabanti who stays in Delhi. Both Shrabanti and her husband (Sunil) saw us off at the airport in the next morning. We reached the Hathorn Airport, London after 10 hours. Suman and Dipti received us in the Airport and took us to their house. It was about 45kms from Airport. The weather was quite pleasant- no heat of Delhi, or for that matter, Bhubaneswar, could be felt there. The road sides were green and full of flowers of various hues. The drive from the Airport to Suman's place of residence was highly enjoyable. Suman informed my daughters (Arati, Shashwati and Shrabanti) and my brothers, sister-in-law and other relations and friend about our safe arrival at London. We enjoyed the various types of eatables and fruits Suman kept for our consumption on arrival.

  Their daily routine kept both of them busy. Suman's day began at 4 AM when he did all the morning chores and walked about 3 km to reach the Rly station to catch the train to his office which was about 60 km. away from his residence. He came back late in the evening. Dipti went to her office at 10 AM and came for half an hour for lunch with us at 1.30 pm. Normally she was back at 6pm. Suman kept some books and other reading materials for us. Besides, we also spent our time watching the TV. Suman prepared our lunch before going to office in the morning. His mother asked him not to do so because, besides straining him so much, the food prepared by him got cold by the time we ate it. Thereafter, she cooked lunch on all days except on Sundays when Suman was at home. In fact, on Sunday, Suman would take me to the shopping mall for weekly purchases. On one of these days in the Mall, someone pickpocketed and took away 50 pounds from my pocket. I came to know of it on my arrival at Suman's residence. However, I liked visiting the malls. Most of the vegetables available here were available there though their sizes and shapes sometimes varied. Some vegetable looked quite attractive particularly the Boitalu or Kakharu. Its size was too big, each about fifty kilos. Before I left London, I got seeds of it to plant at my place in Bhubaneswar. Actually, I did so and everyone got surprised to see the size of its leaves. These were as big as baskets but we could not see anything beyond this stage because an elephant entered the garden at night and ate it up. I was quite shocked and disappointed.

Suman took us to several places of importance in London (Buckingham Palace, Downing Street, Parliament, The river Thames, The museums etc.) and also to some good hotels. Hotels certainly did not interest us. Dipti alone loved hotel dishes. Also, the condition in which some people came for food in the hotels was not as per our taste. We observed them silently. I had, during that short span of our stay at London, some health problems. There was an attack of gout- I had severe pain in my right leg and I could not walk. Therefore, despite the plans which Suman had made for our visit to different places, we cut our programme short and came back. We liked the programme of visit no doubt but what made both of us sad was the way in which Suman worked and the hardship he faced.

Friends, Peers, Happiness and Tears

Some use the terms friend and peer interchangeably as synonyms of each other. Apparently, they are so but there is a clear difference between the two terms. A friend is a person whom one knows well and likes to spend some time with. Friendship is a dyadic relation, it involves series of interactions and reciprocations which facilitate re-examination and modification of beliefs and attitudes. One of the cardinal features of a dyadic relation is reciprocal self-disclosure. Peer, on the other hand is a less intimate relationship which one earns many times during and beyond the student days. Peers refer to persons of the same age, same batch, same abilities etc. so viewed all friends are peers but some peers are friends. Friends are less numerous than peers.

One earns friends and peers at different phases of life. One such phase is student days. I earned some of them in school, college, Universities and work places. I had a few of them during my days in Ravenshaw College. Some of them continued to be so (either friend or peer) during my days as a student of Utkal University at Vani Vihar. Some of them who had their post graduate education outside Odisha continued to be friends but reciprocal interactions with them became deplorably infrequent. Some new ones were added as friends and/or peers at Utkal University.

In Ravenshaw College I had friends and peers in our Honours group. Besides, I had a few friends (like Ashok Kumar Mahapatra, Dinesh Prasad Patnaik, Dandanirodah Misha, Asutosh Mishra, Hari Hara Panda etc.) though they belonged to History, English and other Honours groups. I had a few additions to both of these groups during my student days at Vani Vihar. While in the Department of Political Science, our friendship became stronger and closer. Together, we achieved many things and achieved success. Our days became more fruitful and eventful. We had a feeling that we made some contribution to the subject in facilitating provision for teaching Political Science in more and more colleges. A small group of us (Bhagaban, Rabi, Kumkum, Sarbeswar and me) duly equipped by Prof. S.C.Dash, presented the claim of Political Science before the Minister of Education (Satyapriya Mohanty) and obtained government approval for opening of Political Science in many new and old colleges. Ours was one of the rarest batches of the students in Political Science. The final achievement of the students of this batch has been remarkable, both academically and otherwise. Srinivas joined the IAS, noted debater Hara and Dhruba Sahu as also Sudhakar joined central services, noted Odissi dancer Kum Kum joined Indian Postal Services and later chaired the Odissi Dance Institute. A large number of our batch mates joined the OAS/OPS and Odisha Education Service, Jayakrushna and me joined as university teachers. Kumkum won a Padma award.

Ashok came from our locality (Tirtol), a place at a distance of about seven kilometers from my village. We knew each other before we met in Ravenshaw college in 1961. We visited each other's house and loved each other. Our relations became more mature in Ravenshaw College. Despite his joining the IAS in Himachal Pradesh, we continued to maintain contact and relations till he expired in March, 2019. Dandanirodh was very close to me. He was very frank and cordial. He was friendly with everyone and was harsh to none. During our Vani Vihar days, I accompanied him to his house at Khatbin Sahi, Cuttack at least once in every month. His mother was very affectionate and hospitable. When I started living in my own house at Niladri Vihar, Bhubaneswar, Dandanirodh made it a point to come to me at least two to three times in a month. Sometimes, he was accompanied by Pravat. Both of them spent an hour or two and left me. Prabhat became close to us at Vani Vihar. Being the son of an affluent family, Pravat had a higher than general standard of living in the Hostel. He often entertained us (Ashok, Bhagaban, Rabi Pani, me etc.) with very good tiffin in the hotel at the Rajmahal Chhak. We had to hire two rickshaws from Vanivihar to Rajmahal and paid about five rupees each way per rickshaw.

Town bus service from Vani Vihar to Bhubaneswar was not frequent. Sometimes, we returned by bus. Pravat was highly accommodative. Whenever one of us had some guest in the Hostel, Pravat volunteered to leave his room for the guest and sleep elsewhere at night. This loving friend unfortunately suffered a lot. When I had a serious ailment in April 2017, despite his suffering from the killer disease, Dandanirodh visited me and spent some time with me. Now, these three friends have left for their heavenly abode. Dandanirodh started it in April, 2018, Ashok expired in March, 2019 and Prabhat followed him a few months later. Ashok's last video message "Sukadev, I may not be able to speak to you hereafter" made me nervous and when I telephoned to him, Mrs. Mahapatra from Delhi informed me that thereafter Ahsok was not able to speak. This speaks of our relations. I am now remembering those who have left and those who are still with me.

A Blow from the Unknown

August, 2009 was the worst period of my life. My only Son Suman, a worthy, decent, highly caring, loving and kind one, expired at London. During his days abroad, he talked to us, particularly to his mother at least once every day over telephone and gave an account of what he did and how his life had been in the preceding twenty-four hours. On 6, August, 2009 (Thurs day), he talked to his mother for about 45 minutes and then asked her to give the telephone to me to enable him to speak to me. We talked for about half an hour. He was happy and advised me to take care of my health. It was, about 12 noon. I took my lunch thereafter and came upstairs to rest for a while. I was reading a book. A relation of mine who stayed with me came running and told me that Dipti had, over telephone, given some information to my wife and, thereafter, my wife has remained dumb with tears rolling down her eyes. I came down and contacted Dipti who said that Suman died of cardiac arrest. I felt that my brain stopped functioning. I met the worst calamity of my life. The sky actually fell down on my head. I could neither speak or nor cry. It was a shock which no enemy should get in his life.

It damaged me enormously, killed all my dreams, ruined all my plans and disrupted my future. Everything started falling apart around me. I burrowed into my mind to figure out why what happened did happen. The most important asset of my life disappeared and vanished and why the most meaningful one of my life left me. He talked to me about one hour back. Why did he ask his mother to hand over the phone to me? Did he like to have his last conversation with me? Why so abruptly did he leave us? He was hardly 34 years old. He left me at my old age of 68 years. Why was God be so cruel to me? I could not get any answer to these questions. Perhaps Lord Jagannath punished me for killing someone else's only son in my previous life. If my only son has died prematurely, he must have died as per the desire of Lord Jagannath who, being the supreme Judge in the Highest Court of the universe, has done justice. I remembered one line of the Jagannath Bhajan *"Jagannath Kale Jaa Anath,"* (If Jagannath has made me helpless whom should I appeal for Justice?) and I went on singing this line like a mad man.

A week before Suman expired, he had composed a poem and sent copies of it to his sisters (Shrabanti and Shashwati). This poem was on death and, in that poem, he had argued that nobody should shed a drop of tear at anybody's death, including his. Seeing that from my daughters, I felt as if he could foresee his death that came so close to him and asked us not to mourn for it.

My son, Suman

I could not know the cause of Suman's death. The report which was appended to the dead body said "Cause of death-uncertain, pending Histology and Toxicology". The Post mortem report came to Dipti who kept it. When I approached the Indian High Commission at London to help in the matter, Dipti was asked to give a copy to me and she sent it thereafter. This report was also not clear. It said that it could be owing to cardiac arrest or…… It also said that two tests were to be done (Histology and Toxicology). Histology was not done as per "their request". On enquiry I came to know that unless the wife allowed, Histology was not to be done. I was down with grief. Fortunately for me, I was consistently making efforts to keep my mental calm. If anybody was to be blamed, it was Lord Jagannath, if any body's kindness was sought to get out of the crisis, it was Lord Jagannath. I don't blame any human being.

The dead body reached Bhubaneswar on the 9th day (14 August, 2006) and it was taken to Swargdwar at Puri for cremation. Dipti came one day earlier, stayed at my place with her mother, sister, brother, and a few of her relations till 16th August. It appeared from her behaviour that she probably apprehended trouble from us. God alone knows why she and her kith and kin felt so. Was it owing to what they did? She left for her maternal uncle's place on 16th August immediately after lunch. That shocked and surprised everyone including the relatives who had come to join the mourning.

Met a Spiritual leader

It was in this state of affairs that a sanyasi, known to me for decades, sent for me and explained God's arrangement of things. Since I believe in God, he urged upon me to gladly accept that all these unhappy and painful experiences were as per the God's approval. "Everything, good or bad, happens according to God's will, and, if your son expired at such an early age, it must have been according to His direction. Nothing happens in His ignorance." Sometimes, a soul incarnates at a time for a purpose that serves the agenda of another. "Probably, you were not destined for a son but your fervent appeals and prayers moved the Lord and, as a result, a soul got incarnated to exonerate you from the sin of Aputrik (being sonless is viewed as a sin)." He said, "one is on an eternal journey from the realm of spiritual to the realm of physical and back again. The Jivatma changes bodies. Your son has done so. Besides, how long has this relation been with you? You have come in contact with him for a short duration. In his eternal journey, he must have got several hundreds who were his fathers. Don't you remember Bhagaban Sri Krishna views on this? This experience should not shake your faith in God. The loss of your dear son has caused changes in your day-to-day experience. You don't know why this change occurred and who has caused it. When you see this and embrace this as your living truth, everything in your day-to-day experience will be normal." These words gave me strength and courage to face the tragedy of my son's untimely demise though, I must confess, I am still not able to forget Suman or accept his demise. Putra Shoka (Mourning for the son) is rightly said to be greatest of all shocks and misfortunes. There has not been a single day since that 6, August, 2009 when I have not remembered Suman. He will be with me till I die.

    I know that life is a change but, in my case, it was the cruelest of all changes. Facing such a change is not easy. A well-wisher from Bolangir, who was a senior and respected colleague in the university and Knew me and all members of my family including Suman very intimately, asked me not to lose faith in God. "Don't allow any drift from God and path of propriety. Some people in such situations do so and it does not help in any way. The position from which one looks determines what he is. Try to be closer and closer to God and devote more time to Him." I am doing so but I don't know to what extent I am in the right way.

    I had a feeling that my professional life was adversely affected owing to two factors- Sciatica and a notorious colleague. Sciatica made me un-fit to sit for longer hours and devote adequate time to my research. The notorious and scheming colleague consciously and deliberately went on creating situations where no one could be at his best. I planned to devote adequate time to writing a few more books after retirement. Here Lord Jagannath stood on the way. I lost all energy and confidence and all my creative impulses suffered terrible frustration. I have not been able to successfully concentrate on research. However, spiritual literature has revived me and my morale. These days, I devote some time to reading and writing on issues which interest me. I visit some Universities outside Odisha to deliver talks or help them in their faculty selection process. I am also devoting time in a philanthropic organization (Vikash Education Trust) that provides free education to bright students from financially poor back ground. Assignments from the UGC and other national level institutions also kept me busy for some time. I am also in my own way, providing financial assistance to some school and college going students.

Grand son and Grand daughter

My Young Friends

Playing with friends is a story of the past. These days, it is not possible to play in the football field or in the drawing room. However, mind continues to be a lover of games. It continues to have the desire to play with someone. I have always chosen some friend to play with me. These are mostly, grand children of the family, grand sons and granddaughters of brothers and sisters besides the children of my daughters and nephews. At Present, I have three of them available at hand.

Arati's Son Anwesh has the surname of his family's gotra rather than the surname of his grandfather (Chowdhury Mishra). His name for most members is Anshu but for a few of us, (Myself, my wife Renu, her sister Anu as also my Bhaina) he is known as Noogu. His official name is Anwesh Kaushik. Shashwati's daughter is Ashavari, she is so named by her parents who love singing and the Ragas. However, Suman named her as Tiara- whitest bird of Australia where he was there when Ashavari was born. The two are my two eyes, the apple of every one's eye in the family. Anwesh has given good account of himself as a son, grandson, student etc. He is now a doctor. Ashavari completed her +3 Commerce Course (Capital Management) and now she is serving in an American Company at Bombay. When Anwesh and Ashavari joined courses in the Colleges, playing with them became rather difficult. Both of them are serious students. I was in need of a new friend. Such a friend is now available, he is another grandson, my nephew Srikant's Son. He is about nine years old, very active, talkative and is a high-spirited young fellow. He has a sharp mind. He visits me for a few hours each week and adds so much of energy into my body and mind that it becomes adequate to make me remain happy till he comes again. His name is Shreyans and we all call him Nandu. He sings, dances, delivers speech, does acting, mocks others including his grandfather Ramakant who is also an actor. He also gives me lessons and corrects my spelling mistakes. I send for him whenever I feel bored. Such friends are more necessary than medicines. A grand child is a great gift of God.

… Chapter-III

My Professional Career

My professional career spread over four phases of my service- Utkal University, Berhampur University, Sambalpur University and finally Fakir Mohan University. I began my professional career in the Post Graduate Department of Political Science, Utkal University on 2 March, 1968. My appointment was against a leave vacancy resulting from Raghunath Ram (Lecturer) proceeding on study leave. Since it was a temporary position, I was waiting for a regular position in some other institution. In the meantime, I received an appointment to join the SKCG College, Parlakhemundi. I resigned from the Utkal University and joined there in August, 1968.

Berhampur University

While in SKCG College, Paralakhemundi, I competed for a post of lecturer in the newly established Berhampur University. I was selected and joined there in November, 1968. This was a newly created university with Political Science, Odia, History, Botany and Labour and Social Welfare as the five initial post graduate departments. Departments of History and Odia could have a professor in the beginning but other departments had Readers as Heads of the Departments. Our department had only three faculty members. D. N. Vohra (Retired from BHU) was appointed as a Reader cum Head of the Department of for a period of two years. My friend and classmate Jaya Krushna Baral and me were the lecturers. We managed the department taking assistance from teachers from Khallikote College. The post of Professor remained vacant until it was filled up by Dr. Vina Mazumdar in January, 1971.

Vina Mazumdar's joining the Department promoted an atmosphere conducive to academic development. Born in an elite family (her father was close to Prime Minister Nehru and her paternal uncle R. C. Mazumdar was an eminent historian) and having her Post Graduate and doctoral degrees from Oxford, she became a show piece of the university. She also had the experience of working in the UGC. Various academic activities in the university were initiated by her. She organized weekly research seminars and involved teachers and research scholars of all the Post Graduate Departments. She was a strong advocate of interdisciplinary research. On most of the occasions, she spoke on problems of higher education, national issues and new ideas she had gathered from the books she read. Dr. Mazumdar was quite competent as the Head of the Department. She was a person of ideas and ideals. Each week, she visited the library, borrowed about a dozen books (also gave me a few) with the instruction to discuss the main points in the departmental seminar. She also involved us (me, my friend J. K. Baral from Political Science department, Dr. K. Mazumdar from History and B. S. Murthy from the Labour Welfare Department) in an election study. We had the first-hand experience of empirical method during the elections of 1971.

She took special interest in sending me and

Jayakrishna to national level UGC sponsored Refresher Courses. I attended the 42-day Refresher course at the Gokhale Institute of Politics and Economics. Jaya Krushna attended a similar Refresher course on research methods held in SN Sinha Institute of Patna. The Refresher Course in Gokhale Institute was an eye opener for me and many others. The programme director (Prof. V.M. Sirsikar) was an internationally reputed scholar on behavioralism. Most of the teachers associated with teaching were equally eminent. Rajni Kothari, Y. B. Damley (Sociologist), S. P. Verma (Contemporary Theories of Policies), P. Bapot etc. were some of them. We were introduced to some contemporary theories and research methods. Topics taught included System Analysis, Behavioral and Post Behavioralism, Political Communication, Psycho-Political Analysis, Game Theory, Statistical analysis etc. These topics were completely new to us because our courses in Odisha did not include them. Initially, like most others, I had difficulty in understanding it properly. Prof. Sirsikar could mark it and each day after the guest speakers' talk, he would summarize the talk for us. His expression was excellent and all of us were able to understand the theories hereafter. It was at this stage that I decided to change the topic of my doctoral research which I had got registered in the Berhampur University. I felt that these new ideas should enrich my research. During the programme, we were shown a computer. Prof. Sirsikar was probably the first person in India to undertake election studies. His work. "Political workers of Poona" was a pioneering work in in this regard.

Prof. Mazumdar did not have a long stay in Berhampur University. For personal reasons she wanted to be in and around Delhi. Going back to UGC was the best choice for her. Prof. Vohra's two-year term was over and Dr. Hari Hara Das had joined in the post of Reader. Jaya Krishna joined as a Research scholar in JNU. Dr. B.B. Jena joined as the new professor in the department. In the meantime, I had a communication from the Common Wealth Fellowship authorities that I was being considered for a fellowship. The Vice-Chancellor of Berhampur University Sri R.P. Padhi in the course of his public address expressed that he was glad to say that despite being a new university, its teachers proved their merit. I started receiving communication from several organizations of UK for different purposes. Prof. John Plamenatz of Oxford University agreed to be my supervisor. All this reached an anticlimax when I received a letter from the Common Wealth Fellowship Authority that my name was dropped from the list. This was a big shock in my professional career.

I applied for a doctoral fellowship of the Indian Council of Social Science Research. (ICSSR). Fortunately for me, I was one of the six selected that year. The university granted me study-leave for two years. I was relieved from Berhampur University on 1st. March, 1973 and reached Bhubaneswar on the same day to join as a Doctoral Fellow under my Professor, Dr. S.C. Dash in Utkal University.

Even before getting ready to start doing my research work, as if it waited for my reaching Bhubaneswar, a big political and constitutional crisis came up on 3rd March, 1973. It was directly relevant to my research. The Congress government. led by Smt. Nandini Satpathy was, in reality, an invisible coalition between Congress and Utkal Congress led by Biju Pattnaik. As per the understanding between the two political parties, all members of the erstwhile the Utkal Congress should have been accepted in the Congress since Utkal Congress party had resolved to merge in

Congress. The Congress party however, accepted all except Biju Pattnaik and the decision on Biju Pattnaik was kept pending. The latter felt humiliated and his followers who were accepted in Congress felt uncomfortable. On 3rd March, 1973, seventy-three MLAs led by Biju Pattnaik withdrew their support to Nandini Satpathy government. and submitted a memorandum to the Governor (Sri B. D. Jatti) and claimed to form a new government. The Governor kept the decision pending on the ground that he was on Shiva Ratri fast and as the matter deserved careful consideration, he would take a few days to give his decision. Ultimately, Biju Pattnaik could not form the government. Presidential rule was imposed in the state under Article 356 of the constitution on 5th March. This led to massive political developments. A public meeting of the united opposition was organized on 7th March at Cuttack where Dr. H K Mahatab, Biju Patnaik, Nilamani Routray and many other leaders spoke volumes against the Congress government at the centre denying them the opportunity in forming the alternative government. Since the current political development in the state was in relation to my area of research (coalition politics), I decided to gather as much information as possible.

    I took about three-month time to prepare the schedule for empirical data collection. A copy of the draft schedule was sent to Prof. Rajni Kothari who had promised to help me during my days in the Gokhale Institute at Poona. He made some valuable observations which I incorporated. Thereafter, I did the field work with the interview schedule prepared for the purpose. The sample was purposively random. The respondents included political leaders, bureaucrats, journalists and some senior public figures who had direct or indirect relation with formation or dissolution of coalition governments. Significant among them were Biswanath Das, Harekrushna Mahatab, Biju Pattnaik, R.N. Singh Deo, Nandini Satpathy, Nilamani Routray, Radhanath Rath, Prasanna Kumar Das, Panchanan Tripathy, Somanath Som, Pyari Mohan Mahapatra, Engineer Mumtaz Ali etc. Besides, I also had interaction with Annapurna Maharana, Sarala Dei and Satyabadi Nanda from the older generation people of leadership. I worked in the Utkal University library and the library of the Odisha Legislative Assembly for some time. Finally, I worked for about two months in the Sapru House library, New Delhi which seemed to be extremely helpful. The press clippings section as Sapru House was of immense help to me. The draft of the thesis was finalized in May, 1975 and I returned to my duties in Berhampur University on June, 1, 1975. The thesis was submitted for examination in August 1975 and the results came a year later in Septembers, 1976.

Some Memorable Interactions

In course of doing my field work in connection with my doctoral research, I had interactions with many political and administrative elites. Some of these interactions were very fruitful and unforgettable. Among the political elites whom I had the opportunity to interact with, there were six former Chief Ministers of Odisha. These included Dr. H K. Mahatab, Biju Patnaik, Biswanath Das, R.N. Singh Deo and Nilamani Routray. Biswanath Das was the oldest and seniormost among them. All these leaders had experience with coalition building, maintenance and / or dissolution. Biju Patnaik had wide experience in coalition matters. Even though he was the chief architect of the coalition of Dr. Mahatab (1959-61), he was kept out of the government by Dr. Mahatab. His party (of which he was the leader) was a partner of Biswanth Das coalition of 1971-72. The coalition headed by R.N. Singh Deo had a negative agenda against Biju though ultimately this negative agenda facilitated Biju Babu's reemergence in Odisha Politics, Nilamani Routray had privilege of being in all except Singh Deo Coalition.

I began my field work by interviewing Dr. Mahatab, the grand veteran of Odisha Politics. Besides being my first interview with an eminent political leader of national repute, this interview was in the nature of a pretesting the appropriateness of the interview schedule. Even though I had obtained prior permission to have his interview, Dr. Mahatab seemed unprepared to spare time for this. He became evasive on most questions and tended to get irked. In response to my question on the impact of the coalition on government, he got irritated and said "coalition is at the political level and the government has nothing to do with it". In one of the public meetings of which I had attended, Dr. Mahtab said that governor B.D. Jatli failed in his constitutional duty by recommending for President's rule under article 356 of the constitution when Biju Patnaik with 73 MLAs was ready to form the alternative government. I asked Dr. Mahatab, during the course of the interview, as to what should have been the best for B.D. Jatti. Dr. Mahatab gave a surprising answer, "he has adopted the best course available to him under the constitution". When I reminded Dr, Mahatab about what he had said in the public meeting, Dr. Mahatab replied, "in politics, what is spoken is not always done".

Biju Patnaik was quite frank in his response. He made it abundantly clear that coalition was not a device for taking courageous decisions. At each stage of decision making and implementation, what was uppermost in the mind of coalition parties was political gain rather than peoples' interest or future of the state. On the development of the state, he was of the opinion that unless heavy investments were made for Odisha's economic development, the state would continue to be poor despite rich natural and mineral resources. Commenting on coalition governments in general and the coalition that he practically built, in consultation with Prime Minister Nehru and the Congress Working Committee in 1959 (Mahatab Coalition, 1959-61), he said, "coalition being temporary self-seeking alliances do not have unity of purpose – they distrust the opposition besides distrusting each other. However, it may be resorted to only when it is unavoidable". He said that Singh Deo coalition was based on a negative agenda to expose Biju Patnaik's corruption. This coalition failed miserably and thus it betrayed the electorate. Biju Babu was very critical about Biswanath Das coalition (1971-72) and called it a time-consuming purposeless political alliance and therefore its continuance was abruptly stopped.

Biswanath Das was very courteous in his talk and behavior. When I pointed out to him that Biju Babu referred to his government as purposeless and time-consuming political alliance, he said that it was Biju Babu who did not permit the government to function. He could have become the Chief Minister rather than almost forcing me to be back in politics. He also could have joined the government as a cabinet minister after his election to the legislative. He had one thing in mind and another on his face. He actually ran the government and made it nonfunctional. Biswanath Das was an upright person and he always carried his letter of resignation in his pocket, as he said. Understanding Biju Babu's desire to provide leadership to the coalition, he resigned from the position of Chief Minister but it was Biju Babu and his team of supports who almost prevailed upon him to withdraw the resignation.

Being a very senior leader, Biswanath Das told me of an incident of his childhood days. He and all his batchmates of the school, where from he appeared at U.P. School examination, got plucked. On enquiry, it was found out that all these students failed in the 'dictation test'. On enquiry, it was learnt that the students could not control their laughter in the examination hall when a Telgu speaking Odia teacher uttered an Odia passage for dictation test with the Telgu accent. His peculiar pronunciation made the students role in laughter. This made the examiner angry resulting in failing all the students in the dictation test. The guardians represented before appropriate authority and the examination was re-conducted. "That was the condition of our mother tongue", he said.

R. N. Singh Deo was very calm, friendly and gave his considered views. He had a lot of appreciation for coalitional regimes which provide scope for removal of regional imbalance and opportunity to most areas to be associated with decision-making. As regards impact of the coalitional polities on governing process, he said that it was not peculiar to coalitions only. It also happened in single party government. As regards minister – secretary relationship in coalition governments, Singh Deo held that it always depended on the personality of the persons concerned. However, he had information that some Secretaries did not behave properly with some Ministers. "Once the docile ministers know how to deal with them, there will be proper interpersonal relations."

Nilamani Routray had a variety of experiences relating to coalition or coalition-like situations. As a Minister in Nabakrushna Choudhury government, he developed skill in party management. In Mahatab coalitions of 1957-59 and 1959-61, he mastered the skill in mustering majority on the floor of the House. For that he along with Biju Babu took necessary and timely steps. In the opinion of Nilamani Babu, the worst among coalitions in Odisha was the R.N. Singh Deo Coalition (1967-71) in as much as it had no positive achievement to its credit. It came to power on a negative agenda – to expose Biju and others as corrupt. In that also, it was a total failure. Biju was highly eulogised by the Khanna commission as a leader who was really committed to the cause of Odisha. As regards the Nandini Satpathy coalition, Routray held Nandini responsible for the fall of her government. She forgot the commitment made at the time of merger of Utkal Congress with the Congress. She tried to humiliate Biju Patnaik.

In course of discussion, Routray disclosed a secret to me. It was in relation to government formation after the elections to Odisha Legislative Assembly in 1957. None of the parties had the majority to form the government though the congress was the single largest party. It needed 15 members to have the majority. Dr. Mahatab accompanied by Biju Patnaik called on the Governor who advised Mahatab to take all possible steps to from the government. On return from Raj Bhawan, Biju Patnaik, Biren Mitra and Nilamani Routray forged the signatures of all the seven Jharkhand MLAs and some independent MLAs in a letter addressed to the governor promising their support for Dr. Mahatab to form a popular government. On the basis of this, the Governor allowed Dr. Mahatab to from the government but later, these MLAs bargained with Dr. Mahatab for a heavy price. Routray was directly involved in meeting their demands and ensuring manageable positions for the government until the government was dissolved.

I also had the opportunity to interview Nandini Satpathy. She was evasive and seemed to get irked easily.

She had a very busy time then. Even though I obtained prior permission to meet her in connection with my research, I had hardly adequate time to discuss. She had frequent telephone calls and discussion was often disturbed. At the end of about 3 hours, I had a feeling that I wasted patience and my time.

I had interaction with some civil servants too. Discussion with a few of them was enriching and fruitful. One of them was Somanth Som who was an officer of good repute. He narrated the plight of good people in bad political environment. He had a disciplined moral life. No amount of pressure could deviate him from the path of probity. External pressures have impact on those who in course of doing government job have an eye on their personal interest.

Pyari Mohan Mahapatra (who was then District Collector of Keonjhar) was an intelligent officer. He was not ready to accept that the bureaucrats were less intelligent and less capable than the political leaders. "At least, I do not believe this, unless one deliberately chooses to be involved in dirty deals nobody can force him to such a position" he said in response to the question as to how he countered pressure from the political executive. Mahapatra said, there were upright persons both among politicians and administraters.

I had interviewed one Chief Engineer who was nicknamed as government-maker in view of his popularity in political circles. It was said (rightly or wrongly) he was one of the chief financier to political parties irrespective of whether they belonged to ruling or opposition parties. He was Mr. Mumtaz Ali, a very well-behaved gentleman. I had an interview with him at his residence. I asked him whether the rumor that all politicians / parties sought financial help from him were true and, if it was so, how could he manage it. He said that the rumor was partially true. Some political parties sought his help and he did not hesitate to help when it was possible. He did not pay it from his salary nor did he collect bribe from others to pay it to the politicians. He only conveyed it to some people who needed the help of such people. "Therefore, one person paid and another person took it, though everything passed through me, I am not a party to it".

My final Days in Berhampur: From many points, my stay at Berhampur was memorable. I had good friends and memorable days. I still have relation with some of the old colleagues and students of the department. Since this was a new university and I was one of the seniors most teachers of the university, I felt quite happy and comfortable there. However, I had to leave it to join Sambalpur University in January, 1978 as Reader in Political science. Old friends and colleagues (such as Prof. Harihar Das, Dr. J. K. Baral, Dr. Pramod Kumar Sahu, Subas Pati, Chandrasekhar Panda, B.S. Murthy etc.) continued to keep relation with me. Unfortunately, some of them (Prof. Harihar Das, Dr. Pramod Kumar Sahu, Subas Pati) have already expired.

Some of my old students in Berhampur University also became professors there. Notable among them were Dr. K. S. Padhi and Dr. B. C. Chaudhry. Both of them have already retired. Both of them have proved to be excellent teachers, researchers as also assets to the university. They remember me and telephone me at least once on the occasion of the new year day. The university campus was beautiful and well planned.

Berhampur University was memorable also because of my active role in curbing students' indiscipline. In those days, discipline in top educational institutions in south Odisha was not well maintained. Khallikote College, the most important college of Berhampur, was in a bad shape from the point of view of discipline. Examinations became its worst victim. Impact of this indiscipline was felt when we started preparing for our Post Graduate examinations. Students demanded that they should be allowed to appear at the examination with books. The university community stood firmly against this attempt. Examinees returned from the halls without appearing at the examinations. Examinations were repeatedly postponed. Students got convinced that in no case the university and its teachers would allow books in examination hall. This was one of the worst periods in the university. Criminal elements among the students threatened teachers of serious consequences if they prevented taking books to the examination hall. Being very young and without much experience, we had a lot of tension during this phase.

The most powerful moral force at this critical juncture was the courage displayed by some seniors like Prof. Vina Mazumdar, Prof. Gopal Rath etc. We became firm and did our best to prevent malpractice in examination. Hereafter, the attention of the university was shifted to the conduct of examination in Khallikote college and the law college. Young Teachers of the university, like me, did invigilation work in these colleges and helped in restoration of discipline and sanctity of the examinations.

As young teachers, we observed the way the Vice-Chancellor, R.P. Padhi (Retired Additional Chief Secretary) handled the situation and the skill he displayed in winning confidence of the teachers. For the new university, such a dynamic Vice-Chancellor was a great asset. I was particularly impressed with how he functioned and viewed thing. Needless to say that this helped me very much when I was given the responsibility to build the newly established F. M. University.

Having acquired a doctoral degree in 1976, I applied for Readership in Political Science in Sambalpur University in response to their advertisement and was selected for the post. I joined the Department in January, 1978.

Sambalpur University then

By the time I joined this Department, there were one Reader (Dr. A. P. Padhi) and 3 Lecturers (Brindaban Patel, Dr. Laxminarayan Mishra and S.P. Guru). The Department imparted postgraduate courses in Political Science. Subsequently, a year Later, A P Padhi became professor and Head of the Department. The university started imparting M.Phil Courses and our Department besides teaching M.Phil in Political Science also taught M. Phil in Public Administration, even though no special recruitment of faculties was made. Hereafter, name of the Department was changed as Department of Political Science and Public Administration, I became Professor in March, 1986. Dr. L. N. Mishra became Reader earlier than Brindaban Patel who became Professor earlier than Dr. Mishra. Dr. Radhegopal Pradhan and Subranshu Mishra also joined the faculty. Both Dr. S.P. Guru and Dr. R.G. Pradhan became Professors later.

Brindaban Patel specialized in Political Thought, Dr. A. Padhi taught Indian Politics and Public Adminsitation, L.N. Mishra taught International Politics, S. P. Guru taught Political Sociology, Political Theory and Comparative Politics. I offered the course on Contemporary Political Theory and Orissa Politics.

While in Sambalpur University, I became professor in the same Department in March, 1986 and retired therefrom on 31 March, 2003. During my stay in Sambalpur University, I had gained rich administrative experience as Chairman, Postgraduate Council and, then Director, College Development Council and also as the acting Vice-Chancellor of the university when the Vice-Chancellor Professor Priayambada Mohanty Hejmadi went abroad for some time.

Campus Life: My stay in Sambalpur University was for more than quarter of a century. Nowhere else, not even in my village, nor in my house at Niladri Vihar, I have stayed so long. It is a very nice place and I have many memories, (both good and bad) associated with it. People of this area are good, simple and loving. An ordinary man of this area is an honest and dependable person. It should not, however, suggest that all persons of this region are so. Quite a few of them can be successfully compared to the most crooked people of other parts of the state and country.

The university campus, called Jyoti Vihar is situated besides a hill. The University Library, Guest House and some Post graduate Departments are on the hill. Despite the hills, the campus is well planned. The hills become very beautiful during the rainy season in providing a massive greenery. A variety of trees on and beside the hill presents a beautiful scenery. Different trees (Such as mango, Jackfruit, Sapeta, Orange, Guava etc) grown by the university in staff quarters as also the road side plantations add beauty to the campus. Prof. Bhubaneswar Behera, who was an eminent engineer during his period of Vice-Chancellorship took very active interest in developing the campus. He associated a team of young teachers in this work. The eastern and southern sides of the university campus are covered by a hill. Most of the staff quarters are situated at the foot of the hill.

There were two schools, (one from Class I to Class VII and a High School) in the campus. These were Odia medium schools. Now an English Medium School has come up. There is also a Junior College imparting the +2 Course. I was the President of the School Management Committee for some years. Thus, the campus planners have given due consideration to children's education. The university has a Health Centre. It was not very well equipped, it had one doctor, two Pharmacists and a Peon. The V.S.S. Medical College being close to the campus and the doctor in the Health Centre being an MBBS (with no specification), campus dwellers did not depend much on the Health Centre. People took help of the Health Centre for Pathological test and blood pressure measurement.

In summer the campus was very cruel, we felt highly uncomfortable because of the intolerable heat. My quarters was located on the foot of the hill. Trees become leafless and unable to lessen the impact of heat. Because of the extreme heat, poisonous snakes from the hill came down and the residents felt unsafe. In coastal Odisha, people sleep in their homes at night. During the summer, some sleep outside but not in the open field. In Sambalpur, particularly in the campus, people sleep out side in the open. We were not accustomed to sleeping in the open. However, we sat on a place under the open sky up to about 11 pm and thereafter, went inside to sleep. Rains in the campus were unpredictable. A shower of rains comes suddenly and goes away like this. We therefore, some times, compared an undependable person to the campus rains.

Life in the campus was quite good and comfortable. People had undisturbed academic and personal life. The Bishweshwar Mahadev temple added charm to the campus life. People could have a darshan easily and conveniently. A grand community lunch was organized every year in this temple on the Kartik Purnima. All campus dwellers contributed for it as per their desire and ability. The employees took the trouble of making purchases, arranging cooks and preparing the lunch. All employees (from the Vice-Chancellor to the Class IV Employees) had the pleasure of enjoying this lunch. The food items were not very rich but the lunch was really excellent. I particularly enjoyed the Ambili. This Ambili is peculiar to the Sambalpur area. In the coastal area, taste of this item is, most times, lost because of addition of excess sugar to it. I still remember the Kartik Purnami community lunch enjoyed at Jyoti Vihar. Really unforgettable.

Another such day was the day of Holi Celebrations. Some Professors (Prof. M. C. Dash, Prof. G.B. Behera, Prof. S N Rath etc.) came to the Vice-Chancellor's residence to sprinkle Aveer (holi powder) on him and bring him together to the University Health Centre where people from all quarters and lanes congregated. Here all offered Aveer and greeted each other. There were some naughty ones who brought such powder that its removal from one's head became a problem for 2 to 3 days. One such person was a driver (Pandey). Many therefore, tried to avoid him. All sat together near the Community Centre, planed for a dinner and necessary collection of money was made by some. Holi in the Campus was memorable.

Social life in the campus was very friendly and cordial. It was characterized by sympathy and empathy. Nature of most dwellers was quite good. I remember an occasion where the campus dwellers gave an excellent example of their fellow feeling. A colleague of ours who finalized his daughter's marriage, (including the date of marriage) had, unfortunately, an untimely death on the eve of the daughter's marriage. The family did not have an adult except the wife of the deceased to organize the marriage.

It was at this stage that a group of teachers and other employees came forward, organized the marriage, the feast and everything. We felt proud that our community could do that. Teachers and different categories of employees contributed to make the campus life convenient. When I joined in 1978, I had to depend on Burla Market (at a distance of 3kms) for all grocery goods, vegetables and other required items. Almost all families of the campus purchased their grocery from one shop (called Kumuti Dokan). A brother of this Kumuti had cooking gas shop from where all had their cooking gas. We formed a cooperative society and, through it, had all our grocery goods in the campus. Dr. Ashutosh Nayak of the Department of Chemistry was its secretary. I was also associated with it and sometimes accompanied Dr. Nayak when he went to Sambalpur town to make purchases for the society.

Since I spent such a long duration of time in Sambalpur, I have earned quite a good number of friends and well-wishers. Some of them were senior teachers who had their love for me. I continue to remember them. Some were colleagues, (like Prof. B. Patil and Prof. S.P. Guru) who shared their feelings with me. There were also some from the office. The most numerous among all were the students who had their post graduate education or guidance in doctoral research under me. Many of them still contact me over phone, call on me if they come to Bhubaneswar and send messages on some occasions. As far as I know, in no other profession, people are remembered in such large numbers after retirement.

As the Warden of the Hostels, I introduced some reforms with active support of the then Vice-Chancellor (Prof. L. K. Mahapatra). As Chairman of the Postgraduate Council, I coordinated with the Controller of Examinations on all matters relating to examination dates and dates of publication of results, and thus I acquired the skill in solving naughtiest issues inviting student unrest in the university. As the Director, College Development Council, I had full support of the two Vice Chancellors (Prof D.R. Naik and Prof M. C Dash) and I devised methods of ensuring transparency in matters relating to accordance of affiliation and quality improvement in colleges under the university. Because of my careful management of this office of the Director CDC, the university revenue collection increased several folds and, at the same time, it meant no additional expenditure. Prof M.C. Dash (Vice-Chancellor) associated me with some very confidential business relating to recruitment of teachers. That helped me when I had to do it in F M University. He also associated me in crisis management in the university. These helped me later.

Rotation of Headship: Unlike in foreign Universities, Universities in India appointed a Professor as Head of the Department and he/she continued as such till retirement. In all the universities of Odisha, this practice was in vogue. The Head of the Department was mostly, the seniormost teacher and was viewed with respect by his/her colleagues and students for his/her academic preeminence and experience as also age. He took all major decisions concerning the Department in the Faculty Selection Committee, Academic Council, Board of Studies and in other important committees of the university. Headship was a very responsible position. Because of the dynamic Head of the Department, some Departments made spectacular achievements in getting brilliant teachers, uptodate course of studies, active and hardworking students known for their achievements in the national and international fields whereas some others had hardly any achievement. Nonacademic matters and un-academic activities kept some of such departments busy. None could think of depriving a Head of his position and role. The Act and statutes of the university armed the Head of the department with such powers and a wrong person in this position did enormous loss to the subject, the department and the university

Sambalpur University, for some administrative failures, was superseded by the government in 1989 and a former Professor of the London University (Prof. B.P. Dash) was appointed as its Administrator. As per the notifications, the Administrator could exercise all powers of the Vice-Chancellor, the Senate and the Syndicate. One of the early decisions he took was rotation of headship. As a consequence, I being the second senior Professor in the Department, the headship of the department was assigned to me. All departments in the university had new Heads. There was leadership crisis in some departments but some managed it well. Emphasis now shifted to the department Teachers Councils whom the head of the department had to consult on all administrative and academic matters. This became a process of democratization no doubt, but it had also some harmful effects. Some negligent teachers found it a convenient way to settle scores with the head during their term of headship. Senior most professors who lost their headship due to this new rule did not take the change kindly and some created all possible road blocks.

I became Head of the Department: I became head of the department in two phases, first, when the system of rotation started in 1989 and, again, in the year 2001. The immediate need at the time of rotation was to maintain stability in the department without hurting the feelings of the senior faculty members who felt let down because of this new decision. Some senior professors had grievances against rotation. Except for a few, most of the erstwhile heads of departments understood me well. That made me function at my best in taking help of their experience.

Preparation of the teaching schedule was a very important business. Consultation with all members in the Departmental Teachers Council was made while assigning courses. I ensured that there should be no disruption in the teaching schedule. Classes should not be dropped in any case. In case someone was on leave, someone else should teach from his course in that period. No work hour should be wasted.

Courses were completed and examination held in time. Results were also published as per schedule. Since periodic review of teaching, work load reallocations and readjustments were made according to the discussion in the Teachers Council, there seemed improvement in quality of teaching. Efforts were made for regular seminars by the students and teachers. The Department organized state and National Level Seminars on various issues of topical importance. Efforts were made to ensure larger attendance of students in class rooms by periodically informing their parents and guardians about their absence from class room. The department thus established rapport with the guardians.

Earlier, quite a good sum of money was collected from students for internal seminar expenses and it was kept with the head of the department. Except the head of the Department and the Seminar Secretary who received and spent the money in instalments from the head, no one else knew about the accounts. I heard some murmurs earlier. With the rotation coming into force, we decided to have an elected Seminar Secretary (Cultural) who had the responsibility of organizing different cultural functions including annual picnics in the department. The funds collected from the students were deposited in a Joint Account opened in the bank. It was jointly operated by the head of the department and the elected Seminar Secretary. The expenditure was scrutinized at the end of the session by four student representatives (2 from Part I & 2 from Part II MA Course). This promoted transparency. The surplus, if any left in a session, was utilized in acquiring assets for the department. During a period of five to six years, the department had all such assets required for any cultural activities.

In course of time, the Departmental Teachers' Council became an important agency in developmental activities. A development fund was placed at the disposal of the department and it was used as per the decision of the Teachers' Council. However, in some departments (and even our department at a later stage) management became a victim of democracy.

I became the Director, College Development Council: This responsibility was forced on me by the then Vice-Chancellor, Prof. D. R. Naik. I was reluctant to accept this because I was one of those who were vocal about corruption in it. Scandals relating to these were many. It was alleged that some of those who were associated with opening of a new college, grant of affiliation and further affiliation were not bothered about quality education. Normally, on receipt of the request for opening a new college and grant of affiliation, the university appointed a committee of experts who, visited the college in the university hired taxi, had a physical view of the college, its land records, Bank Account Book, Library, qualification of teachers etc., discussed concerned matters with the college authorities and made recommendation to the university for accordance of affiliation. I tried to locate the points of weakness in the process and suggested the following to the university.

(i) In case it was the first affiliation to a College, the Committee should visit the college in the university hired vehicle, personally have a look at the relevant records and physical infrastructure before making recommendations. None of the members, not even the Director, should take an additional taxi making it obligatory for the college to pay unofficially.

(ii) In case it related to further affiliation, the business should be transacted in the university headquarters. The College, as before, would pay Rs.2000/- as inspection fee and nothing more. The principal of the college and some of his colleagues would come with all documents, Cash Book, Bank Pass Book, Library Stock register, Photograph of all new constructions made and the developments done and such other documents relating to teachers etc. In case the university had any doubt with regard to the presentations made by the college, a new committee would visit the site.

(iii) Instead of the college entertaining the visiting members with lavish breakfast and lunch, the university arranged a plate of tiffin to all members and the college staff, thus eliminating the alleged harassment to the college.

(iv) Sometimes, some members appointed by the university force sell some of their books to such colleges, some deliberately travelled in a separate vehicle and charged the expenditure

(v) The Committee and the college sometimes had a problem when some members dropped in the last hour and caused disruption to the programme. As per the new arrangement. The university appointed all members of the committee but in case any one of them failed to turn up in time, the Director appointed a substitute from out of the list of experts (subject wise) approved by the Vice-Chancellor. All substitute experts were from the university Post Graduate Departments as it was easier to recruit their support immediately. This had another advantage. Neither College nor the member had any prior information about each other and there was no scope for gifts or brief cases.

Two days in each week (Friday and Saturday) were fixed for the purpose. The venue was fixed and time was fixed (4 Pm to 6 PM). Atlast eight colleges could present their cases in a day and decision could be quick since the report was received on the spot.

This had a benefit for the university. The college representatives arrived in the university at their cost, university did not need any taxi for this. Expenses were minimized and the university revenue from this source had 300% rise.

My House was like a Hostel: My wife its Warden

Ever since I worked in the Berhampur University in 1968, I always had one school or college going student staying with me. My adoptive father's nephew (San Bapa's Son Parikshit) was with me for some years and had his school education. When I joined the Sambalpur University, my wife's brother Prashant stayed with us and had his graduate course in G.M. College. He also stayed with us for a brief period when he worked as a Lecture in Burla College. My sister-in-law (Anu) was with us when she worked as a Lecture in the Baragarh Women's College. She stayed with us till she got married in 1983. My Bhaina's Son Banaram had his intermediate and graduate courses in a college at Burla and he was also with us for long four years. Shant, Bhaina's youngest son was with us for some time when he was preparing for some job. My brother Niranjan's daughter Tuhu and son Tapan stayed with us during their Postgraduate Courses in the Sambalpur University. Tapan, however, stayed for another two years with me at Balasore when I was the Vice-Chancellor of F.M. University. He did his M.Sc. Course in the Information Technology in the F.M. University and he thereafter became a Lecture in Information Technology in an Engineering College at Bhubaneswar. Among all these who stayed with us, fortunately for us, some remember the love and affection they had from us. They are reciprocating the same in adequate measure. I am thankful to them for the way in which they take every account of our problems at this age and do their best to make our life comfortable.

Chapter-IV

Fakir Mohan University: Efforts for Recognition

The Balasore Educational Foundation

Odisha had three general Universities (Utkal, Sambalpur and Berhampur Universities) along with one university of Agriculture and Technology. During the regime of JB Patnaik as Chief Minister of Odisha, two more Universities were created (Sri. Jagananth Sanskrit University and Utkal University of Culture). The latter two had specific orientations of imparting education of Culture and Sanskrit. The Utkal University, owing to its size, the area it sought to serve as also the academic branches of education it imparted became unmanageable. Conducting examinations, evaluations and publication of results became a great problem, particularly results could not be brought out in time. The UGC Visiting Committee, in one of its reports remarked that another university should be carved out of it in North Odisha. This comment reached the relevant people and provided necessary basis for a demand to have another university in North Odisha.

A Committee was formed in the undivided district of Balasore (Bhadrak and Balasore). It decided to exert pressure on the government for necessary action. Public demands were made and it led to a movement under the leadership of the former Socialist leader-cum-freedom fighter Rabindra Mohan Das. To strengthen the movement, an organization (Balasore Education Foundation) was formed. Mainuddin Ahmed, a retired IAS Officer became its President. Rabindra Mohan Das became its Secretary & Treasurer. The Foundation had eminent doctors like Dr. Harish Chandra Jena and Dr. Bijay Giri, political and social activist like Maheswar Bag and Prasanna Pal, many Advocates like Sambhu Mohanty, Chandra Kumar Mohanty etc. and retired government officers like Baidyanath Sarangi, Anant Das etc. and an eminent woman activist Dr Radha Devi. Most eminent people in the Socio Cultural and Political life of Balasore and Bhadrak demonstrated their active support for the movement. They represented to the government for creation of a university at Balasore to cater to the academic needs of the four districts of Balasore, Bhadrak, Mayurbhanj and Keonjhar.

The demand for a university at Balasore awakened the People of the adjacent tribal dominated district of Mayurbhanj. They took the tribal dominated Keonjhar along with them and organized another university movement. They held that the undeveloped tribal districts needed a university more urgently than others. Such a university would take care to build human capital appropriate to their genius. Many argued that unless a university was established in Mayurbhanj, imparted education and prepared appropriate human capital, their development would continue to be far off their dreams. This made the position of the government quite difficult.

Balasore-Baripada Divide: Creation of North Odisha University

In order to strengthen their position via-a-vis Mayurbhanj, the Balasore Education Foundation earmarked a plot of seven acres, opened a college imparting degree and Post graduate courses and named the Campus as Vyas Vihar (after Vyasakabi Fakir Mohan Senapati who is regarded as father of Odia prose literature). Regular teaching started in the college and the movement continued non-stop. Just as Rabindra Mohan Das provided leadership to Balasore and Bhadrak, Prasanna Kumar Das, another eminent Socialist headed the movement for a university at Baripada, the district head quarters town of Mayurbhanj. Whereas Rabindra Mohan Das was no more active in politics, Prasanna Kumar Das was still active in ruling Party as a Minister. The government, in order to bring an end to these years-long movements, declared the creation of North Odisha University on 27th Nov, 1998, and appointed Mr. Kshirod Kumar Mohanty as Officer on Special Duty for it. The university's headquarters was temporarily located at Bhubaneswar and it was expected that both contenders would come to a compromise and finalize a venue which would be half way between Balasore and Baripada. The total number of Colleges placed under the university was about 120, making it economically viable.

Creation of the university and deliberately leaving its headquarters for a compromise between the two parties rather than bringing them up together intensified agitations in both of the groups. The then Minister Higher Education, Bhagabat Mohanty was also a former socialist like Rabindra Mohan Das and Prasnn Kumar Das. He used their background of socialist brotherhood and bargained with them for a compromise venue. Nothing worked and both the parties refused to budge an inch. Both pressurised the Education Minister in their favour.

Birth of FM University

In the mean time, there was a change in leadership of the ruling party and state's Chief Ministership. Giridhari Gomango succeeded J.B. Patnaik. Bhagabat Mohanty, as Education Minister impressed upon the new Chief Minister for creation of another university, giving North Odisha University to Baripada and Fakir Mohan University to Balasore. Both the Universities were inaugurated by the Education Minister on the same day (July, 11, 1999) in places of their choice (Baripada and Balasore). However, North Odisha University celebrates its Foundation Day on 27th November. It is senior to F.M. University by about seven months. Prof. Gora Chand Patnaik was appointed as Officer on Special Duty for FM University. Hereafter, he was appointed as Vice-Chancellor for one year. Prof. K.S. Behera, retired Professor in History became the first regular Vice-Chancellor of FM University (17th Sept, 2000 to 16th Sept, 2003). I succeeded him and jointed as Vice-Chancellor of that university on 17th Sept, 2003.

Fakir Mohan University in Sept, 2003.

The university functioned from a three storeyed building donated by the Balasore Education Foundation to it. Out of the total of seven acres of this plot, the Balasore Education Foundation retained one acre and an one storeyed building standing on it, and it donated the remaining six acres to the university. Between the university's three storeyed building and the Education Foundation's one storeyed building, lay a large open space. There was no boundary wall nor even any fence, thus it allowed stray cattles to gather during the day time in office hours. During nights, the open space served as a resting place for the trucks that passed by. There was no pucca road close to the campus or even in the campus itself. There was a tin plate, written on it, "Fakir Mohan University" at the entrance gate of the building. There was neither any reflection of the glory of the great man Fakir Mohan nor any look of a university. The university ran self financing courses on MBA, MCA and Biotechnology with the assistance of locally available part time teachers.

The Infrastructure of the University

There were only three officers (Vice-Chancellor, Registrar and Controller of Examinations). The Registrar acted as the Comptroller of Finance (COF). The office staff included about 10 clerks and four peons. The university had no vehicle of its own, the Vice-Chancellor used one rented taxi and another rented taxi was being used by the Controller of Examinations (COE) as per his official needs. The taxi owners also rented out these taxis to other people during the nights. When I came to know of it, the vehicle was kept at the residence of the Vice-Chancellor at night to avoid possible misuse of the name of the university.

The university had so far not received any land from the government for construction of its campus. It received Annual Block grant from the Government of Odisha to manage itself. There was not much surplus to spend for development. There was no library of the university. The library of the former +3 College of Vyas Vihar was kept by the Education Foundation in two wooden almirahs under their custody. The university had been accorded recognition by the UGC under 2(f) of the UGC Act, 1956 to conduct examinations and bring out the result in the 61 colleges (including two technical colleges which were later transferred to BPUT) within its jurisdiction in Balasore and Bhadrak districts. I realized the enormity of the problems

I would face after I joined as the Vice-Chancellor. For some times, I was scared but I decided firmly to face the problems and solve them. It was a great challenge no doubt but, more than that, it was a great opportunity for me. I felt that I had an opportunity to build an institution for which I should always be proud in my later years. I should build it with all good traditions of advanced universities besides those of the universities I was familiar with. I should also erect safeguards against the problems noticed in some universities during my teaching years. Since I had to start with a tabula rasa and since there were almost none to prevent me from planting new ideas and institutions, I felt, the almighty has favoured me in putting in such a situation. I had quite a good number of loving friends, students and relatives in the state bureaucracy whom I had never approached for any personal favour during my career. That helped me and I could recruit their kind support for the F.M. University and, thus, I started my journey. I realized that I should take immediate steps to make the university eligible for recognition of the UGC under Section 12(B) of the UGC Act, 1956, and make it eligible for development and academic grants from the UGC, DBT, DST etc., so that it could move in right direction.

The F.M. University Office and Officers

After joining as the Vice Chancellor, when I visited the administrative units of the university i.e. offices of Registrar, Controller of Examinations and Comptroller of Finance, I apprehended that such a small group of 14 persons (most of them were very young and without much experience) would not be able to help me in doing anything. However, I did not lose patience. The two officers (Dr. H K Parija- Registrar and Dr. A.K. Panda- Controller of Examination) looked quite confident and competent. I myself had earlier gathered some experience in my earlier places of work - I worked as Vice-Chancellor, Chairman PG Council, Warden of Hostel and Director, College Development Council. Also, as a member of the Syndicate, I had understood the problems of a university and the methods of their solution. I decided to directly know each one of the clerks and the nature of work being done by him. I made it a point to reach the table of any one on any day at any time to know the problem pending with him. When I visited the Controller of Examination, I also knew his problem and helped in arriving at a good decision. My emphasis was on fair and fast disposal of business. Fortunately, things worked well. I knew all the employees and also knew their attitude and talents.

The 10 clerks were distributed among the sections of the Register, Controller of Finance and the Controller of Examinations. Subsequently, the university appointed about 3 clerks on daily wage basis. Besides the government asked the university to accommodate the three former Lecturers of the Vyasa Vihar College in some capacity as per the university need. These three were appointed as clerks. Thus, the total number of clerical staff came to 18. Class IV staff (peons) were about five. These numbers were raised after the university started the five Post Graduate Departments. Most of the clerical staff were sincere and hardworking. I must give credit to them for the way in which they obeyed me and worked on holidays and also beyond office hours and, thus, helped expediting developments in the university.

There were four officers including the Vice-Chancellor. The others were the Registrar, the Comptroller of Finance and the Controller of Examinations. However, the Registrar functioned both as the Registrar and also as the Comptroller of Finance. In view of my experience in other Universities, I had a feeling that it must be a senior officer of Orissa Finance Service who should function as Comptroller of Finance. Dr A K Panda, a Reader in commerce was the Controller of Examinations. I was not worried about him because he was doing the work of a teacher whereas Dr. Parija had administrative work including the naughty finance. However, he worked very well and without any fail.

Dr. Parija was the university's Registrar till he retired from government service on 30th June, 2006. Since a substitute was not available on that date, I appointed Dr A K Panda, the Controller of Examination as the Registrar till a regular Registrar was appointed by the government. He was relieved from this duty on 31st Nov, 2006. During this short period of five months, the university had many problems and functions which Dr. Panda faced quite successfully. Dr. Amulya Chandra Kar a senior Reader in History took over from Dr Panda as the Registrar. Dr Kar and Dr Panda being old friends and colleagues in different colleges, had appreciable cooperation with each other. Dr. Kar continued for some time as the Registrar even after I retired, Dr Panda was transferred to F M College and a substitute joined as Controller of Examinations.

With the increase in varieties of development activities, opening of new Departments Library, Hostels, student activities, Distance Education etc., there was an urgent need for appointment of new staff. Despite my requests for sanction of additional staff, government seemed totally insensitive. The university, therefore, appointed some clerks, peons, Library Assistants, Lab Assistants, Photographers etc from out of its own resources through a service provider. I must appreciate the way the office functioned and facilitated implementation of different programmes in short periods.

Recognition under Section 12(B): The Challenges to be Met

The UGC accords recognition to a university under this section provided it fulfills certain conditions. The sooner these conditions are fulfilled, the earlier the recognition becomes available. I was aware that any failure to take due note of these requirements puts a university in financially semi starvation condition. I concentrated on fulfilling these conditions.

Land: The first condition was that the university should have adequate land in its name for growth and development in future. I pursued the university's request for land in the Odisha Secretariat where I had some of my dear friends and relatives. I met officers of the relevant Departments and solicited their support. I impressed upon them that despite its birth more than four years ago, there had been almost no growth and development. Unless the university became eligible for academic grants from funding agencies such as UGC, DBT, DST etc. the fund, provided by the state government would not matter much. I built a network of connections with all these who mattered for the growth of the university. I devoted major part of the Puja Vacation of 2003 to pursuing the application of the university for land. Things seemed to move quite well. Many in the secretariat had their good will for me and ultimately for the university. In an evening in the last week of October, 2003, I had an experience which I can never forget. I was inspired and excited when Mr. Ramlal Jamoda, the then Secretary, Department of Higher Education was kind and good enough for the university in conveying to me over phone that the state cabinet accorded approval for allotment of 74.52 acres of land at Nuapadhi for FM University Campus. Possession of the land was given to the university in April, 2004, though quite a good portion of that land was under unauthorized occupation.

Creation of 5 Departments: As per the UGC norms, a university should have at least five Post Graduate teaching Departments, with adequate teaching staff. The university had earlier applied for five Departments and 25 Faculty position. The Departments it suggested were Political Science, Odia, Commerce, Physics and Chemistry.

Before I joined, the university requested the government to create 25 teaching posts (one professor, two Readers and two Lectures for each of the five Postgraduate Departments. As regards the subjects suggested by my predecessor, I felt that all these Departments existed in other universities of Odisha and their repetition would not be much in the state's interest. A new university should open windows to new knowledge relevant to the changes taking place in India and at the international levels. I spoke out my mind to the Academic Council in December, 2003 and I was glad that they accorded their full support. We decided to open (i) Departments of Bio Science and Bio technology, (ii) Environmental Science, (iii) Business Management, (iv) Information and Communication Technology and (v) Population Studies. Accordingly, I requested the government to change the subjects suggested earlier by the university. The university went ahead in preparing syllabus. In the department of Biology and Biotechnology, there were some common courses for both the streams of Bio Science and Biotechnology, besides special courses relevant to both of them. The departments simultaneously would produce M.Sc. in two branches of

Biology and Biotechnology. Similarly, in the department of information and communication technology, a student who left the university after completing the 2nd year courses was awarded as M.Sc. in information and communication Technology. Those who continued and completed the third-year course, earned the degree of M.C.A. The courses were duly framed by experts in all subjects.

In the Boards of Studies of Business Management and Environmental Sciences, the university associated experts from industries who identified the needs of the industrial world. A very senior executive of the Infosys was associated with formulation of the M. Sc. (I & CT) and MCA Courses.

I Contacted the UGC and came to know that the "term adequate number of teachers" meant one professor, two Readers and three lectures (not two lectures as suggested by my predecessor earlier) and immediately brought it to the notice of the government and requested them to sanction an additional number of five Lecturers for the university. I frequented my visits to the Secretariat during the period from December, 2003 to April, 2004 and yet the communication from the government sanctioning posts, and approving the change of subjects did not reach me. I expected that a communication relating to this would come any time and I should leave no stone unturned for opening the teaching Department from the next academic session i.e. 2004-05. I started making advance preparation. Besides framing syllabus, I got the draft of the advertisement of posts ready to be sent to the press without any loss of time. An idea unfortunately had come to some people who then mattered in Education Department that teachers of the new universities should be given a lower scale. I was also told so even by the then

Secretary Higher Education. The matter remained pending with this officer for quite sometime.

Kind Intervention of the Chancellor (Mr. M. M. Rajendran)

The more the said high functionary delayed in communicating decision, the greater became my apprehension, restlessness and frustration. Fortunately for me, one affiliated College (J.N. College, Rasalpur) invited the Chancellor to their Annual Function as the Chief Guest and me as the Guest of Honour. After the meeting, the Chancellor wanted to know from me about the problems if any I faced. I told him everything and appealed to him to kindly intervene particularly because the elections to the Lok Sabha and Orissa Legislative Assembly could be announced any time by the Election Commission and, owing to this, no advertisement of posts could be made before June 2004. Selection of teachers and opening of teaching Departments would be delayed. The chancellor who took special care of the universities assured me that I would get the order on the next day. On the basis of this assurance, I convened a meeting of the syndicate for the afternoon of the next day to formally approve the draft advertisement.

This was the day when the first Annual Memorial Lecture on Dr. Harekrushna Mahtab was being delivered by Prof Harihara Das in the F. M. University and, therefore, all notable persons of Balasore and Bhadrak were present there. It was at about 1 P.M. that we received the fax giving details of Departments, number of posts, salary details etc. Except the number of posts, all other things were as per the requests of the university. The number of posts was 25 instead of 30. The syndicate met at 4pm and released the advertisement, indicating that the five extra posts Lecturers would be filled up only after the clearance from the government was obtained. Immediately after our advertisement, came the declaration of election dates. Since no interview could be conducted during this period, the university got the applications processed and scrutinized. I felt that there was a dearth of competent people to scrutinize the applications and provide guide lines as to how to prepare each candidate's career details in accordance with the Act and Statutes. I invited two experienced and eminent professors from another university and got the work duly done. The university also contacted experts and fixed dates for meetings of selection committees immediately after the electoral results were declared. The chancellor was informed about the dates fixed for selection committee meetings. The first selection committee was on Environmental Science.

Selection of Faculties

Just when we were about to start at 10 am, the Secretary to the Chancellor rang me up and said that the Honourable Chancellor wished well for me and expected that I should never deviate from probity under any circumstance. I told him to convey to the Honourable Chancellor that I would always remember the face of Fakir Mohan and not that of anybody else while transacting such business. Selections were made for 27 posts though the university appointed only 22 of them, leaving 5 posts of Lecturers till the government approval was obtained, and three posts reserved for SC & ST could not be filed up owing to lack of candidates suitable for appointment. Appointments were issued in the first week of June and teachers joined thereafter. Two Professors (One of Environmental Science and the other of Business Management) did not join. Immediately thereafter, the university re-advertised the vacant posts. The university took special care to ensure attendance in interview of all candidates, belonging to SC and ST and, fortunately, the three posts were filled up by them.

In this connection, I took a decision which some colleagues wanted me to refrain from. In repeated advertisements, suitable and eligible candidates belonging to Scheduled Castes and Scheduled Tribes were not available for the Department of Population studies. Locally available candidates were far from suitable to be teachers in a postgraduate department. I was worried because unless these posts were filled up, the UGC would not accord its recognition under section 12 (B) of the UGC Act. I advised the Registrar to telephonically contact all SC and ST candidates (besides sending them official letters) regarding the dates of interview to prevent any good candidate's failure to attend the interview owing to lack of communication in time. He did it and, this time, we had quite a good number of suitable candidates. Two of them had very bright academic career and their performance in the selection committee surprised the experts who said "these candidates could have occupied the unreserved posts." I was delighted at their comment. One of these belonged to Maharashtra and other one was from the North-East India. Some one pointed out that they were not from Odisha. I felt that since the university makes all India advertisement, to get candidates from all over India, suitable candidates only should be appointed from all India level as teachers in a university.

Again, the professor selected for Environmental Science did not join. A third interview was conducted and a candidate was selected for the post. He joined in May, 2005. In the mean time, I had a meeting with the Chief Secretary (Mr. P.K. Mohanty) and explained to him that unless the five posts kept pending were filled up, the UGC recognition would not be available for the university. He promised to help in the matter. Necessary clearance came from the Government within the next fortnight and the candidates joined the university. Thus, the thirty teaching posts were filled up.

Developments in the Campus

The boundary and a gate: The university built a barbed wire fence in the Vyas Vihar Campus and made it inaccessible for people taking their plough and bullocks to agricultural field situated in the western side of the Campus. A gate was constructed with appropriate writing on it, indicating that there lay a university. A watch-man was posted at the gate and this ensured that no trucks could halt there at night and no antisocial people could come there during odd hours. However, stray cattle could not be fully prevented, even during office hours. Slight carelessness on the part of the watch man resulted in many of them getting into the campus for grazing and, at the same time, making the campus muddy and dirty. The university had to fix a cattle catcher at the main gate to prevent the cattle from entering the campus.

Main gate of the old campus

Between the university boundary wall (also the gate) and the pucca road, was a stretch of low-lying muddy land which was about 7 to 8 feet wide. During rainy season, huge quantity of rain water from nearby areas made this stretch of land muddy, preventing easy access to the campus. The vehicle could somehow go but the pedestrians had problems. Some bricks and stones were kept in this muddy stretch to enable the pedestrians to cross over. The university did not make bridge like construction to avoid this because it was not sure about its final location.

In this context, I had a very humiliating experience before the experts, from outside Odisha, who had come as members of a Teacher Selection Committee. This was the first day of the selection committee meeting. We had experts from Central Universities of JNU, BHU etc. Business of the Selection Committee was over at about 9P.M. There was a heavy shower of rain in the evening. When all of us came out, our cars could not move in the mud. Some employees placed stones on the muddy patch for the guests to walk the distance. The vehicles came out of the mud only when some of our employees pushed these from the back. I decided to build a bridge over the drain even through it was government land and the audit might raise objection to this expenditure. A contractor of the National Highway obliged us in laying a pucca road of about twenty feet connecting the university gate and the road outside. This was done without a penny spent from the university fund. The contractor who constructed the road also did another favour. The university land was most uneven and undulated. The entire field was full of thorny bushes promoting safe stay and movement of poisonous snakes. The said contractor engaged his people and the JCB to level the land and remove the thorny bushes to make the campus comparatively free from snakes.

The Vehicle stand, Canteen and Bank: Earlier, the students of the self-financing courses kept their two wheelers in front of the building in a scattered manner. This looked very odd. A vehicle shed was constructed in the North-Western Corner of the land alongside the boundary wall to avoid congestion in front of the university office. Situation of the Vyas Vihar campus was such that one had to walk about half a kilometer to get a cup of tea or some tiffin. The students and employees experienced difficulties for this. They could not take any food during the recess. Some of them took unhygienic food from street vendors. I decided to build a canteen and provide necessary furniture and utensils. A tender was floated for the purpose. This decision was very helpful. Sometimes I visited the canteen to see the cleanliness of the kitchen and quality of food. Prices were determined by a committee of student representatives, employee representatives and a few teachers. The arrangement worked well despite change of contractors at suitable intervals. The nearest bank was at a distance of one km and the students and employees found it difficult to go to the bank for their personal transaction during the working hours. I sent for the manager of the UCO Bank. The university had its Account in this Bank and I asked the manager to talk to his senior officer and fix a date for meeting with me for opening a branch in the Vyas Vihar Campus. Their Regional Manager and a few other officers met me and agreed to have a temporary branch for three days in a week in the campus. The university gave them necessary rooms in the ground floor of the office building. Later, this developed into a full- fledged bank.

Mainuddin Garden: The front side of the office-cum-teaching block was empty and it looked quite depressing. Owing to financial constraints and also because the campus was only a temporary one, the university was not in a position to spend money for the beautification. Two gentlemen of Balasore (Himanshu Das and Santanu Pani) donated Rs.50,000/- to develop a garden of flowers. This garden was named after Mainuddin Ahmed (The late lamented President of Balasore Education Trust) who provided guidance to the people to work for educational development of Balasore. The garden was inaugurated by the Chancellor (Shri M.M. Rajendran) on 11th July, 2004.

Finding Space for the Five Teaching Departments

The three-story building donated by the Balasore Education Trust was used for all purposes. Its first floor was used for office. The western part housed the offices of the Vice-Chancellor, Registrar and the Administrative Sections. The Eastern Part was occupied by the Examination wing and the office of the Controller of Examinations. The second floor was used as class rooms and laboratories of the three self financing science Departments run by the university. The ground floor was used as store. There were three halls and three rooms in the ground floor. Since a building suitable for taking on rent for the postgraduate Departments was not available at Balasore. I decided that the big halls should be divided into rooms to temporarily accommodate the Departments. In doing so, we could accommodate two Departments (Biology and Biotechnology and Environmental Science) in the ground floor. Admissions to first year of the self-Financing Courses were stopped and the space hitherto occupied by them was used by the Department of Information and Communication Technology. For the remaining two Departments of Business Management and Population studies, I had a discussion with Dr Harish Chandra Jena, an eminent Member of the

Balasore Educational Trust and the Chancellor's nominee in the syndicate to help in the matter. In fact, Dr Jena was one of those who sincerely wanted that remaining one acre and the building standing on it should be handed over to the university, Otherwise, it would run into wrong hands. I suggested that the university would take the one-storey building on rent for two years @Rs.10,000/- p.m. and pay the entire money in advance and the Education Foundation should construct the first floor on it, so that we could accommodate two Departments there. Dr Jena had necessary interaction with his fellow members and both the parties agreed. The university paid the money in advance and the first floor was constructed in about 3 months time. Thus, the five Departments functioned as per their schedule.

The Library

Library is an important component in a university and the UGC always gives importance to the condition of the university library, its building, books and journals as also the other facilities available to students and researches in it. Prior to my joining the university, Prof. M.N. Das, a former friend and senior colleague of my predecessor had donated a sum of Rs.14 lakhs (from his M.P LAD Fund) for construction of the library building. This money was deposited with the project director, Balasore for the construction work. As per the building plan approved by the university, the work started but the construction took a very long time. My predecessor's three-year term was over but the construction was yet to be over. When I joined, I had a look at the building and found that the quality of work was quite poor. Parts of the building revealed deficiencies. Electrical and PHED fittings were not done. The works, I was told, had stopped for several months. The Project

Director was totally unconcerned about completion of the work. I wrote to the Project Director to complete the work without any further loss of time since the university needed the library very urgently. I also sent a copy of the letter to the District Collector (Mr. Vishal Dev). I talked to the collector over phone and solicited his cooperation in the matter. Within a fortnight, the Project Director wrote back to the university, asking it to deposit another Rs.1.5lakh, so that the work could be completed. He also informed that a sum of Rs.53,712.00 was left unspent with him. When I asked the Project Director the reason as to why the cost of amount 2 lakhs had gone up, he said that there was a change in the plan. This was wrong. The university had no idea with regard to any such change of plan. As per my request, the Registrar sent for a contractor who said that he could complete the work at a cost of about Rs.1 lakh. I requested the Collector to direct the Project Director to return the amount to the university, so that it could complete the work with some private contractor immediately. The Project Director had no alternative and the university completed the work left incomplete. The building was inaugurated by the Hon'ble Chancellor Shri M.M. Rajendran on the Foundation Day (11 July, 2004) of the university.

In the meantime, the contractor (Pravat Biswal) who did the construction work under the Project Director divulged to the Registrar of the university (Dr. H.K. Parija) the cause of the delay in construction, the types of materials used and the bungling made by the Engineer in charge of the work. When I heard about it, I sent for the Contractor. He said that the cement and steel rods purchased for the university library building were used in the construction of the Engineer's house. I asked him to collect details and make an estimate of how much money it would cost. He did so and said that it would be about Rs.1,80,000/-. I felt restless and went on thinking as to how to get back the university money.

The programme for the governor Mr. M.M. Rajendran to inaugurate the library building on 11 July, 2004, was finalized. The District Administration was duly informed by the Raj Bhawan and I also sought the help of the Collector to make the function a success. The Collector visited the Campus to see the arrangements. He visited the library building and commented that the work was not of good quality. It was at this stage that I narrated the whole story which the contractor told the Registrar and me. He asked the Registrar to send the contractor to him. The Contractor, fortunately, fearlessly gave all details about diversion of university resources to the Engineer's house. Then started the excellent management of the situation by the District Collector. He asked the Engineer personally to deposit the amount with the university.

Inauguration of the Library building by the Chancellor (Sri M.M.Rajendran)

The engineer went on repeating his innocence but the collector was very firm. In a meeting in presence of other officers, me and the Registrar, he made it firmly clear that unless the Engineer paid back the Rs.1,80,000.00 to the university by 11 AM of next day, he would place him under suspension and send him to jail. The next morning, the Engineer, through the concerned Contractor started negotiating with the Registrar of the university. He requested for an extension of time up to 4PM. When the Registrar informed me, I refused to be a party to it. He offered Rs 1 lakh and promised to give the remaining amount by 4pm, I did not accept. I made it clear that university would never give a wrong report to the collector who had so skillfully unearthed the university money. He was forced to pay back the total amount to the Registrar by 11 AM. This was an excellent day for all of us. I informed all these to Hon'ble Chancellor during my meeting with him at the end of the month. He appreciated the role of the collector and said that it was a much better method than handing it over to the vigilance.

Electricity Supply

When I joined in the university in Sept, 2003, the office room of the Vice-Chancellor was air conditioned but most of the time, owing to disruption of power supply, it was a horrible experience to sit and transact business in hot summer. The university had a generator (10 H.P) which provided energy for fans to move in the areas occupied by the offices of the Vice-Chancellor, Registrar and controller of Examination. The university had a single-phase electric connection from the GRID and it did not have any dedicated line for supply of electricity. When the experts from famous Universities of India came to the university in connection with selection committees for recruitment of teachers, they had the experience of this extreme heat. When the Hon'ble chancellor visited the university in July, 2004, the need for undisturbed electricity supply was realized and, with kind intervention of the District Collector (Vishal Dev), a temporary three phase line connection was made available to the university. However, immediately thereafter, this facility was withdrawn. The GRID authorities advised that the university should have its own electrical sub-station and dedicated line of supply. Necessary payments were made and we had our own sub-station. Yet, undisturbed electricity supply continued to be a dream. Despite all requests, letters and meetings with the Engineers, there was no improvement in the condition. We continued our efforts.

Healthcare Centre

An ideal university must have provision for health care of the students, teachers and employees. All the good Universities have such provisions. Fakir Mohan university being a new one, and yet to get government grant for a Healthcare Centre, did not have any institutional sanction of funds for recruitment of doctors and other staff. However, the students and employees had their ailments and it was necessary for the university to provide for their health care. I had a discussion of this problem with some local doctors and one of them (Dr. Chowdhury Satyabrat Nanda) a medicine specialist and an eminent doctor of Balasore offered his free services for three days in a week in the afternoon. On other days, if any one had any problem of health, he or she could come to his clinic and get free medical assistance. This system worked well. The university provided a room in the office building and a peon was assigned the duty to be present on the specified days at specified time. Dr Nanda Kept a set of all instruments used for medical check up. He also distributed sample medicines (received by him from the companies) to the students and the employees.

Students Health Insurance

Ours was the first university in Odisha to bring all students under insurance cover. In the year 2003-04, I found that some students had health problems for which they were admitted in private hospital at Bhubaneswar and Cuttack. The university provided them free transport to the hospital but beyond this, nothing more was possible for the university. The syndicate, on my request, considered this and agreed to bring all students under insurance cover. All students were brought under cover of the National Insurance Company for an assured help up to Rs. 1 Lakh. This began with effect from the academic session 2005-06. Other Universities emulated it. Health Insurance of students by the university became an eye opener for many.

Students Assessment of Teachers

The university introduced this right from this first year of regular teaching. It would have been difficult in an older university where critics could be many because it posed a threat to their position and reputation. But there were no problems for me because all teachers were new in the university and they were appointed during my stewardship of the university. Even those who did not like it had to accept it. It is desirable that the teachers should come thoroughly prepared and teach in the class, giving details of development made in their respective subjects. The university provided adequate number of computers to all Departments for use of teachers and students. Therefore, teachers would have no difficulty in browsing and availing the latest developments in their respective fields. Necessary format was prepared by a committee of teachers. Due care was taken to avoid disclosure of who wrote what on whom. Safety of the student was ensured. This pioneering decision had good impact on teaching learning process. The Chairman, Postgraduate Council was entrusted with the responsibility of conducting the business. After each semester examination, this assessment was done in all the five Departments. None of the teachers of the concerned Department was associated with the conduct of the assessment made or the analysis of it. The Chairman had to ensure this. FM University was the first in introducing this system in Odisha. I don't know which other Universities have made such provisions.

Communication Skill Development

For all the five Postgraduate Departments imparting education on professional courses, it was felt necessary that the students should have proficiency in communication. Arrangements were made by the university to provide free training to all Students in communication skill development. Each year, some people like Prof Bibudhendra Narayan Patnaik, Retired Professor of I.I.T, Kanpur, visited our university and imparted necessary skill for two weeks. This benefited the students immensely as was evident from the success of the students in the campus interviews made by different companies. There also, FM University was the first general university to have Campus interview.

Campus free from Students unrest

To ensure an unrest free Campus, I planned to keep the students fruitfully engaged throughout the year and to isolate them from the mischief mongering nonstudents who often visit campus of different universities and illegally stay in the hostels. Besides, the Superintendents and the Chairman, Post Graduate Council sometimes made surprise visits to the Hostels and had details about all that was there in the Hostel. I also, sometimes, while going back from office in the evening, came to the Hostel, talked to the inmates about their food, health, academic problems etc. This method helped me in getting all details, about their difficulties, and before they could ever get organized to meet me, I came to them and solved their problem. If I remember correctly, they came to meet me in an organized way to put forth some of their difficulties for about three to four times. Before they could reach my room, I came out, took them all along with me to the down stairs, sat comfortably and discussed the problems and sorted them out. F M university was the first university to prescribe a special blazer for each student. This distinguished the students from non-students. The university got the blazer for all students tailored and distributed to the students. In fact, the UGC Committee appreciated this very much.

    The other decision to keep the students fruitfully engaged thought out the year was non-negotiable predetermined academic calendar. F M University was the first university in Odisha to take such a decision and firmly implement it. The date of admission, commencement of teaching, semester examinations and declaration of results were notified in the beginning of the academic session and, in no case, these could be changed. This added to the sense of urgency of the students and they had hardly any time to spare for unnecessary things. Teachers also became serious in their business.

Cafeteria approach to Courses

Just as one was free to choose the dishes in a self-service restaurant, the students, after admission to a department in the university, still possessed two papers from other subjects as per their choice, academic or personal. Necessary arrangements were made in the syllabus. Students of Biology and Biotechnology chose some paper of Environmental Studies and Vice Versa. Most Students opted for some courses in information and communication Technology. To facilitate this, the university became pioneer in providing adequate number of computers to each department. A Bridge course was also introduced for students of Biology and Biotechnology who chose to learn Biophysics.

Memorial Lectures

The university started four Memorial Lectures in the name of great sons of Odisha in general and those of Balasore and Bhadrak districts in particulars. These four lectures were: Dr. H K Mahatab Memorial Lecture, Kabibar Radhanath Memorial Lecture, Kantakabi Laxmikant Mahapatra Memorial Lecture and Fakir Mohan Memorial Lecture. Out of the four such lectures, two were delivered by eminent educationist from Odisha (and also from other states) in each of the university campus at Balasore and the Bhadrak College, Bhadrak. This promoted a sense of participation in the enlightened segments of both the districts in building the university. Besides, these were in the nature of showing honour to the great sons of Odisha.

Election to the Senate, Syndicate and Academic Council (July, 2004)

Elections to these bodies were overdue. Quite for same time, there was a truncated syndicate, though this body was quite helpful in building the university. Its members were positive in their attitude. I was glad that these members were different in many ways from many members of syndicates in other universities who sometimes used their syndicate membership as a tool for self aggrandizement. Since the university was preparing itself for scrutiny of the UGC committee for accordance of recognition under 12(B) of the UGC Act, 1956, it should have its own elected bodies (such as senate, Academic Council and Syndicate). Elections to all these bodies were conducted in July, 2004. In 2005, in accordance with the Act and Statutes, the Chancellor completed his nominations to these bodied. The university's syndicate, senate and Academic Council started functioning well before visit of the UGC Committee.

University Journals

The university decided to have its journals, one in Odia and the other in English. The Odia Journal was named as **SAVARNEE** and the English Journal was named as **ANWESHA**. Both of these were biannual. Teachers and research scholars of the university and other eminent persons from outside the university contributed papers to these journals. These were published regularly and as per schedule. By the time the UGC Committee Visited the university in September, 2005, 2 volumes of both the Journals had come out and the committee appreciated the efforts of the university in strengthening research atmosphere and providing motivation for research.

Fakir Mohan National Award in Prose Literature

Fakir Mohan Senapati (1843-1918) was one of the paterfamilias of Indian novel. His works awakened the conscience of the reading public to stark realities of the socio-economic and cultural life of the then Odisha and India. Fakir Mohan was very firmly committed to social justice and had his sympathies for the down trodden and the exploited. As a distinguished Odia man of letters and the first novelist and father of modern Odia Short Story, Fakir Mohan's contributions to Odia, Odisha and Odishan culture is without a parallel. He belonged to an era which was a period of deep unrest and churning. The Odia language faced almost extinction by the manipulators at the administrative level. Being part of the Bengal presidency, the social, cultural and economic life of Odias lay strangled in hostile hands.

As the earliest novelist of India, Fakir Mohan waged a relentless struggle for survival of Odia which was one of the ancient languages. His tone was serious, matter of fact, and forthright. He set the record straight on his handling of affairs, attacking bigotry, hypocrisy and extravagance in Hinduism. His prose vibrating with life is a model for posterity. His language comprising common idiom and popular terms of speech is ubiquitously leavened with many toned human and multi pronged irony.

The university, in order to acquaint the people from outside Odisha with the versatile genius of this illustrious son of Odisha, decided to start in his name, a "National Award in Prose literature", and award it on the Foundation Day (11 July) each year. The first recipient of this National Award was a Malayali Literature M.T. Basudevan Nair. Mr. U.R. Rao of Kannadi literature was chosen in the second year. It was discontinued after I left the university. I am told that this has recently been restarted.

Seminars in the Departments

Normally, Universities get funds from the UGC and other funding agencies for organizing seminars, both national and regional. Since the FM University was yet to get recognition of the UGC under sec 12(B) of the UGC Act, I decided that both the students and teachers should not be deprived of the academic benefit of seminars conducted in the Departments. Besides, the university and the Departments should be academically known outside Odisha. I, therefore, sanctioned a sum of Rs.1,00,000.00 annually for each of the five Departments, from out of our own augmented resources, to organize three Seminars each. Two of them should be National and one should be regional. This should be an annual feature. During the period from July 2004 and September, 2005, each Department had organized about six seminars and had associated many experts from outside in their own Department and Odisha.

Visiting Professorship

I also introduced visiting professorship scheme from our own resources in the Department of Population studies. This Department of the university of Tirupati being an old centre of population studies, I invited its seniormost Professor (Prof. Ram Chandra) as a visiting professor who came and provided guidance to the newly appointed teachers besides delivering lecturers, in the classes for two weeks.

Organisation of Refresher Courses

Even though the university was yet to be recognized and eligible for UGC grant, I could get special permission and funds from the UGC for organizing Refresher Courses in three subjects- Environmental Science, Commerce and Odia in 2004. Three Professors, as Directors of these programmes, conducted Refresher Courses, each for about 40 teachers of different universities and colleges. This inspired confidence in teaches and added to the name of the university. In this connection, the university purchased beds, bed sheets, fans, electric bulbs etc. and took on hire a very big building to provide accommodation to teachers who attended the Refresher Courses. This was done because alternative accommodations in hotels were not available. The expenditure incurred in making these was recovered from the UGC grant, and ultimately, these assets so acquired became assets of the university for use by students in Hostels at a later stage.

Augmentation of Resources

Since the state government's grants were not adequate to develop infrastructure in the new departments, building Laboratories with appropriate equipment, providing chemicals etc. to the Departments and purchasing books and journals for the library, we introduced course fees at the P.G. Level. This enabled us to have facilities and infrastructure which promoted quality education. I have seen in other universities, where I worked earlier that government grants being inadequate, many science departments could not provide appropriate Laboratory facilities. This has enabled the university, even in recent years, to take up different development activities without government assistance.

Joined the Brihaspati Project

The university, having the Department of Information Technology, took special measures to join the Brihaspati Project developed by the Department of Information and Communication Technology, Government of India and the Indian Institute of Technology, Kanpur. The university joined the Programme on 19, September, 2004. Thereafter, an expert from the I.I.T Kanpur Visited the university, installed the system and gave necessary training to all teachers and students of the Department. The students had the benefit of virtual class room arrangement. I do not know anything about this in recent days.

Special Care of Accounts- Appointment of a retired Audit Officer

The Registrar of the university was also in change of the office of Comptroller of Finance. Like me, he was also a teacher and I was always scared that, in view of his lack of experience in financial transaction, he could commit a mistake possessing potential for a crisis. I went on pressurizing the government in Finance Department to post a Comptroller of Finance in FM University. I also requested for immediate appointment of an Internal Auditor who could help the Registrar in disposing cases. Nothing was done for more than two years. I appointed a retired Audit officer of the state government as Officer on special duty (OSD) temporarily. He was of great help to the university in transacting financial business. The new Comptroller of Finance (Mr Singhu Marandi) joined on 23rd. Dec, 2008. As per the advice of the Chancellor (who was a Chartered Accountant earlier), I asked the Registrar to sign in Cash Book after the last transaction of the day. Fortunately, everything went on well.

Planned for a Department of Ballistics

Being a new university, the FM University planned

to have new areas of study which could be professionally and academically rewarding. I had several rounds of talks with the Director, PXE, DRDO, Chandipur (Mr. G.C. Das) on how to start a Department with the support of his organization. Dr Srikant Patnaik, the professor & Head, Department of I and C.T. was always with me in exploring different sources, He browsed in the internet and gave details of a few (seven) institutions providing education in Ballistics at the international level. He downloaded the courses contents. With the help of a group of scholars from outside and some experts from the PXE and ITR of the DRDO, Chandipur, we could tentatively formulate the course contents for M.Sc. in Ballistics to be offered by the university. The PXE promised its full support for this course.

In our proposal to the UGC for recognition of the university under Section 12(B) of the UGC Act, 1956, we included all our assets, infrastructure available, facilities for learning and students welfare as also the specialties of the course contents besides the management of the university as an academic body, its Senate, Syndicate and Academic Council. We also included our proposal for creation of three more Departments (Applied physics and Ballistics, Social Sciences which included Political Science, Economics and Sociology and also School of Languages and literature). For the Department of Social Sciences, we requested for 12 posts (One Professor, two Readers and two Lectures for each of the three stream). Our intention in clubbing different Departments together was to make students familiar with the basics of some disciplines for their success in All India competitions. Similarly, for the School of languages and literature, we requested for 17 posts (One professor and 2 Readers and two lectures for each of Odia, Hindi, Sanskrit and English). Some courses were to be common for all the branches, for example, impact of each language on the other, impact of English on Indian languages, Indian Languages on English, computer application etc. In doing so, we planned to make our products suitable for employment at the national and international levels besides putting therein a solid intellectual foundation. The Department of Applied physics and Ballistics, would add to the national defense besides making its products hot cakes in employment market at the national and international levels.

Visit of the UGC Committee

A committee of experts was appointed by the UGC in August, 2005 to visit the university and examine its suitability for recognition under section 12(B) of the UGC Act. I visited New Delhi, contacted the experts and a date was finalized (1st. to 3rd Sept, 2005). I informed the Hon'ble Chancellor about this date. A very proactive Chancellor as he was, he asked me not to entertain the guests, when they land at Bijupatnaik Airport, in any hotel at Bhubaneswar. He would host a lunch for them in the Rajbhawan. Both the Hon'ble Chancellor and Madam Chancellor were present in the lunch hosted for the guests. The information that the UGC Committee reached Bhubaneswar made the staff, students, and employees of the university (besides the conscious public) quite excited and their happiness was reflected in their behaviour during the committees visit. The actual visit of the committee was made on 2nd sept, 2005.

The students organized a grand welcome (NCC Salute and welcome song). In their interaction with the committee, they pleaded for early recognition and financial assistance to the new university. The teachers presented their Departmental profiles, gave details of their research and consultancy back ground, their equipments in the laboratory, their further needs, Departmental libraries etc. The citizen's committees under the leadership of Rabindra Mohan Das and Dr. Harishchandra Jena met the committee and appealed to it to help complete realization of their dream for a university in the interest of their area. After I presented the case of the university, its assets, infrastructure, its teachers, its new traditions and practices, the committee visited the different Departments.

Discussion with the UGC Committee

On the third Sept, 2005, the committee visited the proposed campus at Nuapadhi. Under the leadership of the Local MLA (Pratap Chandra Sarangi), the locals numbering about 300 people welcomed them with chandan (Sandal) paste, Sindur, garland and sound of Dhol (drum) besides dance and music. The committee was impressed with the type of work done by the university and the need of the area as reflected in the behaviour of the people for a university. It recommended for recognition of the university. The response from the UGC took about three months. I got the message by fax on 23rd Dec, 2005. I faxed it immediately to the Hon'ble Chancellor who was scheduled to deliver his convocation Address to the university on 27th, Dec, 2005.

The Celebrations

This news had wonderful impact on all those who worked with me for this recognition and also for the ensuing convocation. The noted public was inspired and they met me, and expressed their goodwill for the university. While enthusing the employees to work sincerely with me to make the university suitable for recognition, I had promised a lunch/dinner to them. Now that the objective was achieved, I gave a sum of Rs.5000/- to the Registrar to arrange things in consultation with the employees. Dr Harish Chandra Jena offered another Rs.5000/- to the Registrar and requested him to make arrangement for a grand dinner. The employees arranged it and invited, besides all teachers, the noted public who helped the university in many ways.

Chapter-V

Post Recognition Developments

The Post-recognition Problems

While according recognition, the UGC did not sanction any grant. It only made it eligible for grants depending upon its projects and their acceptance by the experts of the UGC. While visiting the UGC, I was advised to prepare plans and projects of the university for consideration of the UGC. Since the Tenth Plan period was to close by the end of 2006-07, the sooner the university submitted its proposal, the better for it. Otherwise, it would not get any grant in the Tenth Plan. I appointed a committee of teachers besides associating myself actively with it. I also consulted some of older colleagues in other universities in finalizing the development proposals for Rs.21,03,32,380.00 for the remaining part of the X Plan. This development proposal included request for Building, Equipments, Staff quarters, Hostels etc. besides the proposal for the three Departments, of Applied Physics and Ballistics, Social Sciences and Languages and Literature, in Feb, 2006. I had to frequent to the UGC to pursue appointment of the committee and its visit to the university. The committee visited the university in April 2006. The UGC Sanctioned a sum of Rs.95,00,000.00 on 24th August, 2006 and asked the university to complete its utilization by March, 2007.

The components of grants were: (i) Lab equipment, computers and peripherals- Rs.72 Lakhs, (ii) PG Text Books and Journals for the central Library- Rs. 16 Lakhs and (iii) Others (Sports, Health Care, Transport, Academic Activities)- Rs. 07 Lakhs. I took expeditious steps in utilizing the grant in accordance with the Accounts Manual. Science Departments purchased equipments and chemicals, computers and other accessories as per their requirement and priority. Two multi gyms (one for the Men's Hostel and the other for the Women's Hostel) along with their accessories were purchased and temporarily installed in the P.G. Department of Population studies for use of the students. Hitherto, the university did not have a vehicle of its own and the vice-chancellor had to use a hired taxi. Another hired taxi was used by both the Controller of Examinations and the Registrar. For both of these taxis, the university had to incur heavy expenditure each month. The state government did not sanction any grant for purchase of a vehicle despite my repeated requests. In all meetings held in the Raj Bhawan and the secretariat, whereas all other Universities had their vehicles for the vice-Chancellors, and also for the Registrars and controller of Examinations, my university had none. Sometimes it had a humiliating impact. I remember that I had to cancel an important business owing to the failure of the taxi arriving in time. Also, I was often reported by people that this taxi carried other people and marriage parties at nights to earn some extra income. With the approval of the UGC through re-appropriation, I purchased a car in December, 2006 from out of the UGC grant.

Purchase of Books

For purchase of books, the university invited tenders and one of the Book sellers of Balasore agreed to provide 30% discount on printed prices. That being the highest, the university allowed it to supply books. This book seller could hardly supply book worth Rs.90,000/- in three months. This gave rise to apprehension that he would not be able to supply books worth Rs.16 Lakhs within the stipulated time. The syndicate blacklisted the supplier and re-advertised. Hereafter two other suppliers were appointed for the purpose. They agreed to provide 26.5% discount on books published in India and 22.5% on those published outside India. We became successful in utilizing the entire amount within the stipulated period and submitted the Utilization Certificate to the UGC by 31 March, 2007.

The Special Experience

The Chairman, UGC (Prof. Thorat) visited the Raj Bhawan. As per the direction of the Hon'ble Chancellor, all Vice-Chancellors and relevant government officers attended a meeting Chaired by the Chancellor to discuss problems of universities of Odisha and how best to solve them.

Prof. Thorat indicated the new directions in which the universities should advance and focus their attention. He held that the Universities in Odisha failed to avail the benefits provided by the UGC because they did not submit development proposals and, even when such projects were financed by the UGC, the universities failed to submit utilization certificates in time. As such, they lag behind universities in other states. He promised that he would send a senior officer of the UGC to guide the Universities in a meeting in presence of the Hon'ble Chancellor. This meeting was held in November, 2006. Mr. A.K. Dogra, Joint Secretary of the UGC came and explained the projects which the universities could easily prepare for immediate finance. A Professor of the university (Dr. B.M. Otta) accompanied me to the meeting. While Mr. Dogra explained the types of projects which the UGC would immediately finance, Dr. Otta busied himself with his laptop in preparing the projects there. We completed seven such proposals which were handed over to Mr. Dogra when he left for Delhi. Al these projects were cleared by the UGC in about 3 months. We had new facilities.

The F M university completely utilized all funds so sanctioned including the book grant of Rs 16 lakhs. Except Sambalpur university which utilized about 50% of the Book grant, no other university crossed 20% of this grant. In fact, everyone, including Mr. Dogra asked me as to how I could do so in such a short period of time. I told them that I had made a special effort in sending the second in command of each of the departments along with the Book Supplier to New Delhi (Daryaganj, where hundreds of publishers were available) to shortlist books relevant to their courses and the Department Teachers' Council finalized the list thereafter and due process of purchase was followed. In fact, we spent about Rs 6 lakhs more than the UGC paid us. Whereas other universities, (except Sambalpur University) got 10% to 15% discount on printed price of books, we got 25.5% on books published in India and 22.5% for those published outside. The chancellor appreciated this proactive role played by me.

The X Plan allocation utilization and after

The university seemed to win appreciation of the UGC for its efforts and performance. Timely utilization of the grants and submission of utilization certificates

impressed the UGC. As a result, we had a shower of grants in April, 2007. These were as follow.
(i) A special grant for development (Rs 14.25 lakhs)
(ii) A special development grant for updating the Management Department (Rs 40.50 lakhs). Out of this an amount of Rs 12 lakhs was to be utilized in the financial year 2007-08 itself.
(iii) An amount of Rs 38.8 lakhs was sanctioned for updating the Department of information and communication Technology. An advance of Rs.31,04,000.00 was received.

The university took prompt steps immediately. Orders for equipment worth Rs.8,09,275.00 for Management Department were issued in April and those for Rs 3.8 lakhs were issued in the first week of May, 2007. The CPWD was entrusted with the responsibility of extension of the Management Department (Rs 15 lakhs).

Out of the Rs 38.8 lakhs sanctioned for updating the Department of ICT, an advance of Rs.31,04 lakhs was received by the university and immediately, thereafter, orders for equipments worth Rs 23.76 lakhs were placed. Besides, the university issued tenders for Rs 10 lakhs for purchase of soft ware.

The CPWD was asked to construct the Women Infrastructure Building. The university had its University Science Instrumentation Centre (USIC) with the UGC grant of Rs 5.87 lakhs. Also, it organized a six-day workshop (26 March-31 March, 2007) in Collaboration with WRIC, Mumbai and gave training to science teachers of colleges and universities as to how to handle scientific instruments and how to repair them. The Department of Biotechnology, government of India sanctioned a sum of Rs 20lakhs for development of Bio Information Centre to promote teaching in Biology. Orders for equipments worth Rs13.5 lakhs were issued.

Preparation of the development proposal for the XI Plan

UGC invited development proposal for the XI Plan. The university prepared its plan for **Rs 66.4766** crores and submitted the same in April, 2007.

New Departments

We requested for UGC Support for interdisciplinary learning programmes. These Were: (i) Natural Resource Management, (ii) Computational Mathematics, (iii) Applied Chemistry, (iv) Sports and physical Education, (v) Film Fashion and Theatre, (vi) Languages and Literature, (vii) Social Sciences, (viii) Applied physics and Ballistics and (ix) Library and Information Science.

While still continuing efforts to have the Departments of Applied Physics and Ballistics, Social Sciences and Languages and Literature, I decided to continue it alive in case I failed to get it done by the government before the UGC Committee for the XI Plan visited the university. However, out of these three Departments two (Applied Physics and Ballistics and Social Sciences) were approved by the Government and were opened in 2007.

Distance Education

Distance Education provided by the IGNOU, through its branches every where, benefits millions of people who could not get higher education either because of lack of resources to pursue it or other difficulties. Many branches of professional and meaningful education were imparted by the IGNOU and the other Universities which were authorized by the Distance Education Council, New

Delhi. Besides promoting education in their areas, the universities also earned quite a good sum of money which they could utilize for their general development. After joining as Vice-Chancellor of FM University, I came to know that there was no such arrangement for imparting distance Education through the university. The university had applied to the Distance Education Council (DEC) to permit it to start Distance Education.

I consulted the Chairman, Distance Education Council (Prof Rajsekhar Pillai) over telephone and requested him to kindly accord approval to the proposal of our university. Quite promptly came the approval from the Distance Education Council. A retired Principal of FM College (Dr. Debendranath Jena) joined as its director. He was asked to take steps to acquire the reading materials from IGNOU and start the programme. After about sixteen months, I reviewed his performance and found that, by that time, he added only Rs.10,000.00 to university revenue. The programme did not succeed in attracting adequate number of students. By that time, the university had its own teachers. One of the faculties of the Department of Population Studies (Dr. B. M. Otta) was appointed as the Director. He chose to work on honorary basis. He was very active, calm, hard working, honest and highly innovative.

The university submitted proposal for grants to the Distance Education Council which sanctioned Rs 30 lakhs for infrastructure development. Reading materials were purchased by the university for IGNOU at concessional rate. Normally, a discount of 10% on printed prices of the materials is allowed by the Distance Education Council. Since the FM university obtained 26.5% discount from all Books sellers, I requested the chairman Prof. Pillai to do a special favour of granting that discount to this new

If Memory Could Speak | 171

University and he allowed it. The university's proposals for preparation of teaching materials in the university was also accepted by the IGNOU and a sum of Rs 10lakhs was sanctioned to meet the expenses. The university organized a Three-day workshop on how to prepare the materials. About 20 teachers from different colleges were invited to attend and be equipped in the matter. Two Professors from IGNOU imparted training to them and thereafter, we prepared teaching materials for some new courses both in English and Odia. When professor Rajsekhar Pillai addressed the Convocation of the university in 2007, he also inaugurated the Distance Education Centre of the university and recognized it formally as affiliated to the Distance Education Council, New Delhi.

Development of Distance Education Programme benefited large number of students of Odisha. We opened several study centres. Care was taken to see that the programme was on proper track. Examinations were conducted in established government colleges and university squads visited examination centers to ensure discipline and sanctity in the examinations. The university could generate an annual income of about Rs 2.5 crores. This helped it improve the infrastructure facilities and facilitated development activities of the university.

Distance Education Round Table

Distance Education branches in University's Development

The university did not have a Conference Hall to hold meetings, seminars, workshops etc. All these were being managed in the small class rooms. With the construction of the Management building at Vyas Vihar Campus, a big hall was temporarily earmarked as the conference hall. It was in this hall that Prof. Rajsekhara Pallai inaugurated the university's website of Distance Education Centre. To make the Hall suitable for such a programme, the Distance Education Branches offered to contribute special funds to the university. Instead of paying any money, they offered to supply suitable chairs, tables, fans, lights, air conditions, screen etc. They purchased things and deposited the same in the university. The syndicate recognized their contributions in detail and thanked them for the materials donated by them. All such materials were also recorded in the stock register. Similar was their help provided earlier in 2006 when the university completed construction of the first floor of the Library Building from out of its own resources. All infrastructure materials were donated by the Distance Education Branches. One could see very active participation of these branches in building a new university and adding to its excellence.

A Printing Unit in the University

Sometimes, examination programs in some universities get disrupted owing to disclosure of question or failure of the printing press in supplying question papers in time. Since we started with semester system at the P.G. level, our examinations were frequent and owing to our own predetermined non-negotiable academic calendar, we felt that the university should have a printing unit of its own. We had it and necessary training was imparted to the clerks, peons and even some teachers to act in emergency situation. We also planned to print our own Journals in this press.

Undisturbed Electricity Supply

The problem of electricity supply continued. It became acute when the departments started functioning. Laboratory works of students, research scholars and teachers were affected. The university had a generator (10 H.P.) which hardly supplied energy sufficient for the Administration Block. A new generator (20 HP) was purchased and both the generators could meet the emergency needs of energy for all departments and the Administration Block. A shed to securely place both the generators was constructed near the electricity substation behind the library building.

Updating disposal of pending degrees and diploma

As is well known, almost all Universities in Odisha have a common tradition of keeping disposal of degrees pending. Students, sometimes, take ten to fifteen years to get their degree certificates. Some even fail to get them when they forget details of their appearing at the examination. Some universities avoid conducting annual convocation. As a result, the students get harassed. When I joined the FM university, as many as 10,598 of such diplomas were yet to be prepared, signed and disposed. The then Chancellor Mr. Rajendran was familiar with these problems of the university. He started alerting the universities. Some of them had more than one lakh such pending cases. I took expeditious steps, got these diplomas and degree certificates prepared and distributed to candidates through their colleges. By the end of my fist term, I was up to date in this matter.

The New Campus: The Initial Challenges

A Highly Complicated Land: The state Government allotted an area of 74.63 acres in the village Nuapadhi. This vacant land lay between two parts, of one village Nuapadhi. The land was used by the villagers for various purposes. There were ponds which they used for bathing, part of this land was used as the village cremation ground and another part was used as play ground for the young boys and girls. Since agricultural land lay on both sides of the vacant land, villagers moved with their ploughs and bullocks through this vacant land from both the side, or else they had to take a round-about route of an extra Kilometer. The land was also used for their daily defecation since private latrine was then a dream. Besides, about 25 families belonging to SC and ST communities had made unauthorized construction of dwelling thatched houses, kitchen garden etc. on this land. An agriculturist, whose land lay close to the university's land, encroached about two acres and had grown big trees in the boundary, thus giving evidence of his occupation for several years. Besides a pucca road connecting the two parts of the village was built by the government in the middle of the university land.

The Role of the Tahasildar: The Tahasildar (Dr Pratap Mishra) demarcated the land, identified the border and gave formal occupation of the land on behalf of the district administration. This occupation was incomplete in as much as the encroachers were not vacated. The said agriculturist refused to accept the demarcation made by the tahasildar. The 25 SC/ST families continued to occupy the university land though the tahasildar repeatedly promised to get them shifted to another place within fifteen days. He tried to impress upon me that he would manage to shift the SC/ST families and the university should not precipitate unnecessary crisis. The SC/ST families insisted that they should be given land before they vacated the present site. The Tahasildar went on making false promises to them and also to me. Nothing worked.

The Chancellor laying the foundation stone of the new campus

This continued for about six months. I made several trips to this place to find a solution. I realized the trick of the tahasildar who wanted to avoid the unpleasant situation of forcively throwing out the SC/ST encroachers without allotting alternative site. I insisted that it should be done in a month's time; otherwise, I would bring the matter to the notice of the government and the Chancellor. I came to know that he was already under orders of transfer which he was avoiding to disclose to me. I brought it to the notice of the collector (a new collector had joined) and requested him to take immediate steps to get the land vacated from the illegal occupants. In the mean time, the government allocated a sum of Rs 4crores for the infrastructure development of the university. The Hon'ble Chancellor (Sri Rameswar Thakur) advised that in view of the experience of Utkal University (quite a good portion of its land has been occupied by more than 300 illegal families) all universities must take steps to protect their own land. He asked me to immediately construct boundary wall to avoid future encroachers.

This was a period of great tension for me. I asked the MES (Military Engineering Service of Defence Ministry) to complete construction of the boundary walls. We started with the southern side walls for which there was not much objection from any side since it was close to the road. Troubles started with construction of the western side walls. The agriculturist who occupied about two acres of university land destroyed the constructions in the nights following the days of construction. We reconstructed the walls and the miscreants repeated their behaviour. The university filed a FIR in the Remuna police station and requested the S.P. (Balasore) to help in the matter. Somehow, we completed that portion of the western side. Next to this side lay the pucca road constructed by the government facilitating movement of people from one end to the other. There was resistance from the villages. I asked the contractors to construct the north western side walls where I expected that there would be no resistance. Here also problem started. Groups of village youths would stop the contractors building the walls. The work came to a standstill position. I had no way out except firmly requesting the District Collector to take steps in the matter. The District administration sent its own personnel and demolition of houses started. Immediately thereafter, about a thousand people from both sides of the village and from the adjoining villages under the leadership of the local MLA (Sri Pratap Sarangi) offered resistance. Some demonstrators even slept before the JCB of the contractor. Pratap Sarangi threatened that there would be bloodshed of the most horrible type if the university built boundary wall and evicted these people who have lived here for decades. I had to stop the work.

The Problems taken to Raj Bhawan

The conference of the Vice-Chancellors of all Universities convened by the Chancellor was scheduled to be held the next day. The meeting was presided over by the Chancellor. Three ministers (Educations, Finance and Revenue) were present. Also about a dozen of secretaries and all the Vice-Chancellors were present. I raised the issue in the meeting and gave details of how the unauthorized occupants, villagers of both sides and the Local MLA made it a political issue and how the work had been suspended following threat of bloodshed.

The matter was discussed thoroughly and the Chancellor requested the Revenue Minister (Mr. Harichandan) and Secretary, Revenue to take up the matter with the Collector, Balasore and find out an early solution to the crisis in order to enable the university to complete construction of the boundary walls. This was followed by a meeting convened by the District Collector inviting the Sarpanch, Ward Member of Nuapadhi Panchayat, local MLA, some other village notables and me. The meeting lasted for more than one hour but no decision was taken. Hereafter, a new collector (Dr. A.C. Padhiary) joined and he suggested that the university should take a decision at their end, hinting thereby, the university should, somehow, accommodate them.

The university convened a meeting of all the stake holders. We met under the shade of bamboo grove in the encroachers' occupied university land. I had, with me, the Registrar (Dr.A.C.Kar), Controller Examinations

(Dr.A.C.Panda), a few employees of the university and some representatives of district administration led by the new tahasildar (Mr. Sambit Nayak). The villagers reiterated their demand and their stand. I made it clear to them that since the government had given the land to the university for its campus, it would not be possible for anybody to stop it at this stage, whatever, may be the situation. My position was clear. I did not have much discretion in the matter. What I could do was to deal with the problem with a humane heart and try to lessen your problem, not eliminate it. I would not go beyond the Laxman Rekha. For this I should get your full support. In case you are guided by others, I would hand over the matter to law-and-order authorities and the state government. The choice is yours. If you accept my words, I will provide some solution here and now. The university would ear-mark an area for the village cremation ground and temporary settlement of the 25 SC/ST unauthorized Occupants. A passage way would be allowed by the university to move from the eastern part to the western part and vice-versa. Farmers could move with ploughs and bullocks also to their agricultural fields. This passage must be closed at night to prevent trespassing. A passage of four feet width would be allowed close from the outer side to the western boundary. This would be 200 meters, connecting it to passage referred to earlier.

    The villagers realized the situation and accepted the suggestions. As per this understanding, the district administration redrew the map in making some minor changes to defuse tension. About 0.75 acre of land in the North-Eastern part of the land was spared for the village cremation ground and resettlement of the SC/ST families. A passage of 4 feet width and two-hundred meter length in the North Eastern side of the boundary wall was allowed.

The passage was open during day time only. It was to be closed in the evening to prevent trespassing and insecurity. The villagers could move from one part of the village to the other and, also, they could go to their agricultural fields with their plough and bullocks. Their demand for the cremation ground was fulfilled and the situation seemed normal and conducive for construction work.

The Last Kick

Hardly after a fortnight of peaceful construction work, there was a heavy shower of rain and rain water of the village which, earlier, was released through the university land before construction of the boundary wall, flooded some houses in the eastern side. I visited the site and realized the enormity of the problem and the threat it posed again to my objective of getting the construction work done. I took help of the lady Sarpanch and her husband and solved the problem. We kept a part of the pond water open outside the boundary wall. This made the situation normal hereafter, some local elements started problems with the contractors, asking them to purchase construction materials from them, asking for booties failing which, they started finding faults with the construction work as self-styled overseers. Some anonymous petitions were also sent by them to the Vice-Chancellor for enquiry. The university lodged FIR in Remuna police station in the names of particular individuals and took help of the superintendent of police in controlling the situation. The Engineer's expert committee examined the veracity of the complaints and found them untrue.

Agency for construction work

The government of Odisha sanctioned a sum of Rs 8crores for construction of the university campus – its building and roads. By this time, the university had decided whom to entrust the construction work in view of he urgency to have buildings built in time and with principle of probity and transparency. During my days as a teacher in other universities, I had an impression that many good vice chancellors lost their reputation when they undertook some construction work. The agencies failed to deliver in time and the Vice-Chancellor was maligned. The responsibility of construction should be given to such an agency which would complete the work in time and without violating the norms of probity and transparency. I had a personal discussion with the chancellor (Sri Rameshwar Thakur) on this issue. He appreciated my attitude and advised that quality of work rather than economy should be emphasized. In the mean time, I visited the I.T.R. (Chandipur) in connection with opening an M.Sc course in Ballistics. I was very much impressed with the architecture and quality of its construction work. The Military Engineering Service (M.E.S.) of the Defence Ministry made all these constructions. I felt that the university should select such an agency for the construction work. I brought the idea to the Syndicate. A committee of the Syndicate visited the I.T.R. in March, 2006 and, after having first hand information on the work there recommended that the university should request the MES to take up the construction work. Negotiation with the MES started, its Chief Engineer (placed at New Delhi) with some other officers visited the university and work site and agreed to take up the responsibility. They prepared a draft MOU which the university got examined by a committee of some professors and legal experts before it was presented to the Syndicate on 24, March, 2006. It was agreed that the university would deposit the entire amount of Rs 8crores (Sanctioned by the government) in April-May, 2006. The

MES would complete the work by 2007 failing which the contractor would pay penalty. I was in touch with the Chancellor on this matter and he said that since MES was a part of the Ministry of Defence, Government of India and its quality of work was well known, entrusting the work of construction to it would be a good idea.

The Bhumipujan ceremony of the new campus

The Syndicate approved the draft Memorandum of Understanding (MOU) unanimously. The MOU was signed and the university informed the government (Finance Department) about this decision before receiving the sanctioned amount. This decision was not liked by those who felt that they would not be able to derive any benefit out of this. A local agency of the state government approached me personally and requested me to reconsider the issue. It should be entrusted to that agency which could do the work and give extra benefits to the university and, all these, at al lower cost. When I said that the university was already committed, he got a letter of recommendation from a Cabinet Minister of the state government, advising me that it would be better if we gave it some state government agency. Similarly, the Minister of Higher Education, in course of discussion, advised that the work should be entrusted to the P.W.D. of Odisha government rather than the MES above whom nobody would have nay control if it faulted. I replied to both the Ministers that I had already informed the government of Odisha (Finance Secretary) about the agency of construction with whom the university has signed the MOU. The Syndicate has already approved everything and any effort by me to make any change might give a wrong message. I was therefore helpless.

Appointed Engineering Expert Committee

Since the work of construction was entrusted to an outside agency, even if it was government Department, it was necessary for the university to have some agency to oversee the work and also to examine whether the quality of work was as good as was promised and whether the progress of work was as per expectation. The university had no staff of its own to supervise the construction work. I appointed a Junior Engineer (Pravat Ranjan Jena) to visit work-site and keep me informed at the end of every day. A committee of Engineers (three retired Chief Engineers of Balasore and Bhadrak districts) met every month, visited the work-site, made enquiries about different matters and examined them. Mr Yadav, the Military Engineer who was in charge of the construction submitted monthly reports containing details about the work done, its proportion in relation to the total assigned work in percentage, its financial cost etc. These were verified by the expert committee and the university sent monthly report of progress to the government for its information as per the reporting by the expert committee. The chancellor was also informed about it in my monthly report to him.

Needless to say, that I visited the work site both in the morning and in the evening to strengthen the sense of urgency in the minds of the contractors besides keeping them under watch. Sometimes, the Registrars (Dr. H. K. Parija) and subsequently Dr. A. C. Kar accompanied me.

The government of Odisha sanctioned a sum of Rs. 8 crores in 2006 for the university to enable it to develop the campus. An important rider attached to this was that the university should utilize it during the same financial year. Otherwise, this failure would have impact on allocation of funds in the next financial year. We started with projects worth Rs 12.5 Crores. These included buildings of the Departments of Bio Science and Biotechnology, Population Studies, applied physics and Ballistics, twelve Teacher's Quarters, roads etc. By the end of the financial year 2006-07, we had utilized more than that. The next year allotment was Rs. 5 crores but we started projects, which along with the incomplete ones amounted of Rs. 19 crores. We started the new Administration Block and the Main Gate of the campus. The UGC funded for the PG Hostels for Men and Women. All these simultaneously were being constructed. The evenings were very beautiful in the campus with the newly constructed beautiful roads, and the Halogen Lights fitted by the MES. In-fact, many people from nearby areas came to see the Campus in the evening. When I saw some such people standing on the road side to see it, I felt delighted.

Ideas to open new Postgraduate Courses

Ever since my joining the university in Sept, 2003 when the Citizen Committee of Balasore accorded a very hearty welcome to me and requested me to open a

Department which would be appropriate to the coastal district of Balasore and the famous ITR (Interim Test Range) at Chandipur. I was exploring different possibilities. Right from 2004, I was in regular touch with the personnel in ITR and the PXE (Proof and Experiment Establishment), the two branches of DRDO, government of India. I had, fortunately, a friend (in PXE) of my attitude. He was Mr. G.C.Das, Director PXE who agreed with me that since this establishment worked at Balasore for more than a century and since Balasore had its contributions to it, in fitness of things the PXE should contribute to the cause of Balasore and Odisha in collaborating with FM university for opening a course peculiar to the genius available here.

After some rounds of discussion, we decided to open M.Sc course in Ballistics. Taking help of the internet, we found that Ballistics was taught in seven universities at the international level and nowhere in India. My colleague (Prof. Srikant Patnaik, Head, Dept. of Information and Communication Technology) collected details about the courses taught in those centers. A committee of experts consisting of Prof Krutibas Patnaik and Prof. Naresh Ch Mishra of Physics Department of Utkal University, Prof. N.Das of I.I.T., Kanpur, Prof Swadhin Patnaik of Sambalpur University besides Mr.G.C.Das (Director, PXE), his colleague and Deputy Director, PXE and few others from the ITR were engaged in working on the Syllabus of the proposed course. They met twice in the university office and decided to have three-day meeting at the PXE head quarters at Chandipur. Mr GC Das offered hospitality to the committee at Chandipur in the DRDO Guest House for three days. Prof. Srikant Patnaik worked with them. Ultimately, the committee said that it should be course on Applied Physics and Ballistics, and accordingly, the course was structured.

The University- PXE Dialogue

By this time, we had no idea that the UGC had approved our proposal. To strengthen our claim for the XI Plan, the university decided to start teaching the course at PXE office at Chandipur. The PXE agreed to spare space, engage its ballistics experts for teaching, allow the students to use some Lab facilities and ballistics related materials and provide free transport to students commuting from Balasore every day. The university agreed to appoint one Lecturer in Physic another in Mathematics to teach the Physics and Mathematics part of the Syllabus. The PXE would donate a Sum of Rs 20lakhs to build the new Department.

The university agreed to reserve 8 seats out of 16 for employees or relation of employees of the PXE. Course fees collected by the university would be utilized in meting the expenses. Post of a Lecturer in Physics was advertised and the university was about to select candidates when Mr GC Das (Director PXE) informed that objections to this arrangement were in some high places. In this connection some name, like Mr Nataraja (Scientific Adviser to Defence Minister), Mr Sibatanu Pillai (Controller of DRDO) were heard. I was shocked but not frustrated. I got a copy of the report of the UGC Committee that had visited earlier and was thrilled to learn that the committee approved our proposal for creation of three new Departments including Applied Physics and Ballistics. I decided to take up the matter with the state government for creation of these three Departments. My Proposal and the report of the UGC Committee were sent to the government of Odisha for necessary action at their end.

In the Convocation organized by me on 27th Dec,

2005, We had Dr A.P.J. Abdul Kalam, the President of India who worked for about 4 decades at Chandipur and had immense love for Odisha in general and Balasore in particular. While welcoming the Chief Guest and presenting my report in the Convocation, I appealed to His Excellency to help FM university realize its dream of having an M.Sc Course in Ballistics. The Chancellor (Shri Rameshwar Thakur) also made reference to this request of mine. Dr Kalam asked me on the Convocation Pandal itself as to how he could help. I told him that the problem could be solved if he kindly said a word or two to the relevant people in DRDO in favour of our proposal. He was extremely kind to say "I give my word of honour". That emboldened and energized me.

Dr. Seelva Murthy delivered Kantakabi Lecture

In the mean time, I came across a very eminent scientist of the DRDO. He was Dr W. Seelva Murthy, the distinguished Scientist and Head (R & D), DRDO, New Delhi. I was fortunate to get his consent to inaugurate a National Seminar on Environmental Protection organized by our Own Department of Environmental Science. He inaugurated the Seminar and delivered the Annual Kantakabi Laxmikant Mahapatra Memorial Lecture at Vyas Vihar. He was highly impressed with the Labs and equipments, of the Departments of Biotechnology and Environmental Science, particularly because the university was a new one, hardly seven year old. Impressed with the type of research work being done in the Departments and the way in which the university, despite difficulties, made efforts to create an atmosphere conducive to learning, Dr Seelvamurthy advised the teachers of both the Departments to prepare research projects and submit to the DRDO for funding. In course of my introductory address in the seminar, I solicited Dr Seelva Murthy's kind help for our proposed Department of Applied Physics and Ballistics. In the lunch hosted by the university for the distinguished guests in the Konark Guest House at Chandipur, Dr Seelva Murthy praised the efforts of FM university for introducing a regular course on Ballistics and said that the DRDO would extend all possible help to the university in form of books, equipments, teachers etc. He asked the top scientists and officers present at the lunch to dump materials needed for Ballistics teaching in the university. *In the initial years, the university would find it difficult to get qualified teachers to impart courses. To address this problem the DRDO at Chandipur must get experts from I.I.Ts and other centers of DRDO on duty and enable the students to have them as their teachers in the class room.*

Solicited kind intervention of Dr. Kalam

To facilitate approval from the DRDO authorities who reportedly had reservations on our plan of joint collaboration (the PXE at Chandipur and FM university) in starting Ballistics Courses, I found it totally essential to seek the blessings of the Hon'ble President, Dr APJ Abdul Kalam who, earlier (on 27.12.2005) on the convocation pandal, gave me his "Word of honour" to speak a word or two to the DRDO authorities at Delhi. Simultaneously, I met the Chancellor who, then, was in charge of the office of the Governor of Andhra Pradesh and gave details of the problem and also what I did. He said that the President would visit Hyderabad on 22 Nov, 2006 and he would talk to him in this regard. He asked me to be in touch with his Secretary (Mr Gopal) in Andhra Raj Bhawan. I interacted with Mr Gopal. On 22 Nov, 2006 when I tried to remind him at 8AM, he replied "already done".

I received an invitation from DRDO for their

conference scheduled to be held on in November, 2006 and this conference was to be inaugurated by the President of India. I was sure that, our Chancellor would be present in the conference and also many high functionaries of DRDO, including the Defence Minister's Scientific Advisor (Mr. Natarajan). I decided to attend it and see if this would help me in my efforts. I had the approval of the Chancellor to be at Bombay for three days but while booking my Air ticket, I booked my return ticket for 29th Nov, 2006 (and not for 1st. Dec, 2006). On my way to the Bhubaneswar Airport, the Principal Secretary to the Chancellor (Mr. N. Sanyal) conveyed the Chancellor's desire that I should come back to Balasore on 29th November and attend the DRDO conference at Chandipur and meet him there. I told him that I had already planned that way. "That is why the Chancellor loves you so much"- he commented. I attended the DRDO conference at Chandipur as per schedule. After the meeting was over, the Chancellor told me that he had already done the work. He took me to Mr. Natarajan who said "your work is done". I requested him to authorize Mr. GC Das, Director, PXE to coordinate and he said that he had already done that. Thus, full cooperation of the DRDO was available to the university.

The proposal for Applied Physics and Ballistics with the government

Even since the university submitted its proposal along with UGC approval for opening of three department, I must have met the commissioner-cum-Secretary, Department of Higher Education at least for ten times. Right from the beginning he seemed opposed to it. Maybe, he had an M.Sc. degree in Physics and he understood things better. He knew all the prospects of the subject. Applied Physics and Ballistics did not mean anything important to him. Our proposal for the Department of Languages and literature was for a composite Department: English, Hindi, Odia and Sanskrit. Besides making our products intellectually sound, an MA degree in one of these subjects in such a Department could have ensured jobs to the products at the national and international employment markets. Besides, the university named after Fakir Mohan would have provided for postgraduate teaching and research in Odia and English. The idea did not win appreciation of the secretary who said that it would add only to the unemployed world of Odisha.

The third Department of Social Sciences was another composite Department providing thorough training and experience in interdisciplinary studies. Its components were Economics, Sociology and Political Science. The Semester-I course was compulsory for all three branches. These included 5 paper Computer Application, Globalization, Theories of Economics, Theories of Political Science and Theories of Sociology. Carefully structured, the courses included all that a candidate for All India services (including the Civil Services) should know about. This is first of its type and its objective was to equip Odisha students adequately for the all-India services. This was not appreciated by the Secretary. He was opposed to creation of all the three new Departments. I met a few top bureaucrats of Odisha who had social science background and who were really worried owing to the declining rate of success of Odisha students in All India Services. One such person was the then Chief Secretary (Shri Ajit Kumar Tripathy) who, for more than a decade earlier, consulted many academic and administrative stalwarts to find out remedial measures to undo Odisha's miserable plight.

In a meeting of all Vice-Chancellors convened

by the Chief Secretary, the needs of all the Universities were discussed. People present in the meeting included the Secretary Higher Education, the Principal Secretary, Finance and a few more officers of the Finance Department. When the need for my university were presented by me, the Secretary Higher Education opposed them tooth and nail. He rejected the demand for the Department of Languages and Literature as also social sciences. When he pooh poohed the importance of Applied Physics and Ballistics, I objected and said "the UGC has approved it, the state government does not support it, please reconsider this request". He replied "Who is the UGC?" to this I said "God alone will save higher education in Odisha" where the Secretary Higher Education does not know who in the UGC. With this, I walked out of the meeting.

This incident gave me a great shock and my impulses suffered severe frustration. I could not reconcile with the idea of pocketing the insult and continue in office for the remaining period of my term. I thought of resigning and bringing the insensitive behaviour of the Secretary Higher Education to public. I decided to write a letter to the Chief Secretary about the arrogance of his Secretary (which was evident from his behaviour and action in the Chief Secretary's presence) and appeal to him to reconsider the claims of FM University. There was no reply to this for about 15 days. It was very painful for me and I decided to resign from Office. I met the Chancellor (Mr Rameshwar Thakur) and offered to resign in view of the way in which the claims of FM University were rejected. He was shocked since he was a supporter of the idea of composite Departments, particularly the idea of Department of Applied Physics and Ballistics for which he lobbied with the President of India and the Defense Minister's Scientific Advisor Sri K

Natarajan. He said "I will not accept your resignation, take it back. Give me a copy of your letter addressed to the Chief Secretary." I gave a copy and came back to Balasore. After about 15 days, I rang up the Principal Secretary to the Chancellor (Mr. N. Sanyal) to enquire if the Chancellor had taken any kind step in the matter. I was delighted to learn that immediate steps were taken by his secretary as per the desire of the Chancellor. The letter emphasized at creation of these new departments in the interest of Odisha and he asked the government for appropriate action.

I got a copy of this letter and met the Chief Secretary who was always positive in his ways and behaviour. He asked me to prepare a draft which he proposed to present to the Chief Minister for his consideration and approval. I had already prepared one, with certain changes it was presented in a week. Both of us sat together, he made some changes, promised to take action and asked me to stop bothering about it. However, he could not take steps for about a week. On enquiry, I was told that he wanted to further modify the draft. When I met him again, he asked me to accompany him to the Minister Higher Education (Mr. Samir Dey) for discussion. Mr. Dey suggested that instead of the Chief Secretary, he himself would sign the draft and present it to the Chief Minister directly. Accordingly, the draft was further modified and signed by the Minister, Higher Education. All the three of us met the finance minister (Mr. Prafulla Ch. Ghadai) who was convinced of the need for creation of such Departments in Odisha's interest. He agreed to send it with his recommendations to the Chief Minister. Ultimately a high-level committee meeting attended by the Finance Minister, Education Minister, Chief Secretary and the Principal Secretary, Finance was held on 10, Feb, 2007 in the Odisha Secretariat.

After discussion on various aspects of the courses applied for, it was decided to create two Departments- (i) Applied Physics and Ballistics and (ii) Social Sciences. Eighteen posts for both the Departments were created and I was asked to go ahead with advertisement for admission of students and recruitment of teachers. This increased the number of PG Departments of FM University to seven, though teaching was imparted for M.Sc. in Bio Science, Biotechnology, Information Technology, Environmental Science as also Applied Physics and Ballistics under the science stream and MA in Economics, Political Science, Sociology and Population studies under the humanities stream besides the MBA whereas some other university which started earlier remained unchanged.

The Aftermath of the decision

I stayed back at Bhubaneswar for a day and carried the government order for necessary work in the university, The press and electronic media gave very wide publicity to this decision and particularly, everybody seemed to be very happy to know of the novel course on Ballistics. People seemed to have peculiar ideas about it. On my way back to Balasore on 12, Feb, 2007, I had several telephone calls from different media representatives who enquired about the Ballistics Courses, its implication from national defence point of view, who should be eligible for this course and how would the products be useful to the society etc. Besides, some also asked me several technical questions which frightened me. On my arrival at the university office at about 4PM, I tried to transact some official business when a former student of mine (Prasant Kumar Mohanty), who was also a Lecture in a local college, met me and said that a Secret Service Officer of Defence Department was waiting to meet me in connection with the introduction of the Ballistics Course. The said officer, after discussion expressed his satisfaction with my replies. He said that he was asked by the Defense head quarters to get the necessary information. It was reported in the press on the next day that some people at Delhi also enquired at the DRDO and Dr W. Seelva Murthy had replied to them that the *products of the Department would be of great use from national defense point of view. The Department of Applied physics and Ballistics of this university would act as the "Knowledge Creation Centre of DRDO".*

PG Dept. of Applied Physics and Ballistics

I do not have any idea about how the Department and the university have maintained relations with the PXE at Chandipur and how the Products of the Department are treated in the employment world. The PXE and DRDO agreed to provide many facilities and provided research grants to some Departments besides paying the relevant amount of money for institution of Gold Medal for the First class First of M.Sc. examination in Applied Physics and Ballistics. I am told that with the change of headship of both the PXE and the university there was lack of coordination. It is an important link which is in the interest of the university and in no case should the link be weakened. The President of India and the Chancellor of the university had a great role in creating the department.

I failed to have the Department of Languages.

I was still not satisfied because my dream-Department of languages and Literature was not created. I approached the Chancellor to kindly intervene. In my presence, he requested the Revenue Minister (Mr. Hari Chandan) to take it up with the Department of Higher Education and find out the way to create the said Department in F.M.University. I made several visits, met all possible people and ultimately failed. My successor probably did not take it seriously. I am glad to know that the university has now the Department of English, Odia and Urdu. It should have Department of Sanskrit.

The Convocation of the University

Even though the university was established in July, 1999, till I joined in September, 2003, there was only one Convocation held, though as per norms, each university should have its Annual Convocations. As a result of this, steps to prepare the degree certificates, diplomas etc were not taken seriously. More than 10,000 students waited for degree certificates and diplomas. Along with the several other steps which I considered necessary to make the university eligible for recognition by the UGC under the section 12(B) of the UGC Act, 1956, I took steps to clear the pending degree certificates in batches. The first convocation

which I was able to organize was on 27th Dec, 2005.

Second Convocation with the President of India Dr. Kalam

I wanted that this university should be known outside Odisha soon and, for this, I planned to have the President of India (Dr APJ Abdul Kalam) as the Chief Guest. Dr Kalam conveyed his consent on 16th Dec, 2005 and on receipt of the President's message of Consent, the Chancellor asked me to meet him on 17th Dec, 2005 to finalize the arrangements. In the meeting, the Chancellor asked me to ensure completion of construction of the boundary wall of the old campus besides the other things. This was essential, as the Chancellor said, from security point of view. Before leaving for Balasore on the next day in the morning, I came to see my 99 year old ailing father who had lost his consciousness for about 24 hours at the residence of my brother. I was afraid that it could be my last opportunity to touch his feet. Had not the President's visit been finalized, I would have stayed back. I had no option in the matter. I reached Balasore at about 11 AM and remained engaged in preparing for the President's visit. A meeting of the syndicate had been convened for the afternoon of 18th December. I made the syndicate aware of the steps which the university should take before the President's visit. With regard to construction of the boundary wall in the old campus, there was a technical problem which the Syndicate solved in consultation with a retired Executive Engineer. The retired engineer said in such an urgent situation the whole of boundary work should not be entrusted to one contractor because we did not have adequate time to make any advertisement inviting tender. On the other hand, the work can be divided among many contractors in an urgent situation like this. As per this, the work was assigned to some contractors to complete all constructions by 25th Dec, 2005. District administrations help was solicited. I returned to my residence at 9 pm.

My father expired

Hardly did I complete my evening puja. I had a telephone call from my brother saying that father's condition was improving and I need not worry about him and concentrate on my official business. Suddenly, he cried aloud and said "he has left us". I could not decide what to do. I rang up the Registrar (Dr. H. K. Parija) and the Controller of Exam (Dr. A. C. Panda) to inform them about it and sought their advice whether I should leave for Bhubaneswar to have the last darshan of my father, join the party to Swargdwar (funeral ground) at Puri and be back in the next night. Both of them advised like that. It was at this stage that my brother telephoned and advised me to concentrate on duty and leave everything regarding father's ritual to him. My wife informed that she had already sent her younger brother and my daughter (Kulu) to reach my brother's place and help him in arranging things. She asked me to busy myself in the preparation for the convocation. I could not sleep for the whole night. I was unfortunate that I was not with my mother and my adoptive father when they breathed their last. I also could not be present at the time of my father's death. I could not be at Swargdwar. Tears kept rolling non-stop from my eyes. The days were awe-fully busy ones. The worst problem concerning the convocation was the security requirements prescribed by the then District Collector. All teachers, officers, some members of the Balasore public life who knew of my father's death, came forward to offer their help. The Honorable Chancellor (Mr. Rameshwar Thakur) learnt about my father's demise and was extremely kind to telephone me, console me at father's death and enquired whether he should send some officers from Bhubaneswar to help me. That gave me immense strength in such a situation. One of my friends, (Late Profulla Chandra Mishra) who was Additional Director General, Police visited Balasore in connection with the President's Visit. It was of great help to me. Also, Mr. N. K. Sundar Ray, RDC, Cuttack visited and gave fruitful suggestion. These visits lessened the difficult security provisions prescribed by the District Collector. The convocation was held on 27th Dec, 2005. The Chancellor (Mr. Rameswar Thakur) presided over it. The President Dr. A.P.J. Abdul Kalam, as the Chief guest delivered the convocation address. The Chief Minister Mr. Naveen Patnaik attended the convocation as a Guest of the university. The university honoured an eminent Gandhian, freedom fighter, a former socialist leader and President of the Balasore Education Foundation Mr. Rabindra Mohan Das with an Honorary D.Litt. degree. Dr. A.P.J. Abdul Kalam was a very popular name at Balasore and his elevation to the highest office of India was a matter of great satisfaction for them. His joining the 2nd Convocation of the university as the Chief Guest made every one happy. The students were very happy that they were awarded degrees in presence of the great President of India, who also after the convocation address, had a brief interaction with them. The convocation was over by 11AM and, immediately thereafter, from the university itself, I left for Bhubaneswar to attend the 10th day rituals (Dashaha) of my father's death. My period of mourning was a period of responsible duties which my father had always tried to impress upon us.

The Third Convocation

The third Convocation was held on 7th January, 2007 and the Chief Guest was Prof. Rajsekhar Pillai, the Vice-Chancellor of Indira Gandhi National Open University (IGNOU) New Delhi. He was also the Chairman of the Distance Education Council, New Delhi. Besides delivering the convocation Address, Prof Pillai inaugurated the newly constructed building for the Department of Business Administration in the campus of Vyasa Vihar. Since 2003, the university had opened Distance Education Centre but a website of the university on Distance Education was yet to be created and inaugurated, we synchronized the inauguration of the website of the university's Distance Education Centre with the Convocation. Prof. Pillai also inaugurated a National Seminar on Distance Education in the afternoon. The university awarded degrees honoris causa to three distinguished citizens who excelled in different walks of national life. They were Prof Manoj Das, Mr. Sarat Chandra Maharana and Mr. Nityananda Mahapatra. The convocation was a grand success except in one thing. The Honorable Chancellor who took every possible step in the interest of the university and was a permanent source of inspiration for me could not attend the Convocation to preside over it and admit the students to their degrees owing to an accident and subsequent serious illness of his son at Delhi. As Vice-Chancellor, I had to play

his role.

Prof. Manoj Das being awarded honorary degree during the third convocation

The fourth Convocation: New Campus Inauguration

The fourth convocation of the university was held on 23, Feb, 2007. The Chairman of the University Grants Commission (Prof. Sukhdeo Thorat) became our Chief Guest and delivered the Convocation Address. By this time, we had a new Chancellor in Mr. Muralidhar Chandra Kant Bhandare who Presided over the Convocation and awarded degrees. This Convocation awarded D. Litt. (Honouris Causa), LLD (Honoris Causa) and D. Sc. (Honouris Causa) to people of national and international reputations. They included (i) Justice Arajit Pashayat (then an Honourable Judge of the Supreme Court), Prof Sukhadeo Thorat (Chairman, UGC), Prof. Prabhat Patnaik (an Economist of international repute and then Chairman, Kerala State Planning Board) and Dr. W. Seelva Murthy, Distinguished Scientist and Head, DRDO (R&D), New Delhi.

Unlike the earlier Convocations, this Convocation was held in the new Campus (at Nuapadhi) which was inaugurated by Prof Thorat on the same day. I had taken steps to build a permanent Convocation Pandal in the new campus. It was fully financed by the contractors engaged by the MES for construction of the new campus. Many buildings in the campus needed completion but a few (Such as the Population Studies Department, the university gate, the 12 Teacher's Quarters etc.) were complete. The Chancellor inaugurated the Population Studies Department and the gate of the campus. The Staff Quarters were put to use on that day.

Campus Sanctification

Since the Campus was constructed on a cremation ground (Smashan), some in the university community opined that there should be some puja to make it fit for human habitation. I accepted their advice and arranged an *Asta Prahari* (24 hour singing of the Mahamantra-Harekrishna Harekrishna, Krishna Krishna, Hare Hare, Harerama Hareram Rama Rama Hare Hare). The university did not incur any expenditure on account of this. I paid some money and the ghee necessary for Haban and the remaining expenditure was borne by the contractors and the MES personnel. The place was sanctified one day earlier than its official inauguration as FM University Campus.

The Campus was so beautiful, the beautiful soothing

breeze of the evening and the well constructed roads with halogen light and the newly constructed building made it highly attractive. Every evening since Nov, 2007, I visited the Campus and planned to shift to it after its formal inauguration. I also motivated some teachers to join me in the new Campus and try to develop this Campus in making it green and clean. However, the inauguration was delayed to 23, Feb, 2008, it was hardly 20days before my date of retirement. Hereafter, for more than two years, the newly built campus remained idle. It was towards the close of my successor's tenure of office, the university shifted to the new Campus. About seven years after I left the university, the new campus remained almost idle. It was Prof. S.P.Adhikari who shifted to the Campus and took steps for further improvement. His successor Prof. Madhumita Dash stayed there and took steps to make it more livable. The present Vice Chancellor, I am told, also stays in the campus and tries to make it more attractive.

Preparation for NAAC Accreditation

One of my desires was to get the NAAC accreditation done during my period of stewardship of the university, particularly because the newly built campus was beautiful enough to impress any outsider visiting the university. Our teachers had, by this time, given good evidence of their hard work in research and consultancy. Also, the good traditions built by the university and the students' record of success in campus interviews added to the reputation of the small university. However, it was not possible to complete the work before I left. Had I about a year to go before retirement, I could possibly have got the work done. The university was accredited with B+ grade during the Vice-Chancellorship of Prof. S.P.Adhikari who succeeded two others after me.

Efforts to acquire more land

The land given by the Government to F.M. University was 74.3 acres. It was not adequate. Besides, the shape of the land was such that it looked quite odd, part of it being quite broad and another part being shockingly narrow. If things go well and the university gets the leadership of 10 active Vice-Chancellors, the area of the land will pose problems for its future growth and development. In course of adjusting with the hostile environment while building the boundary wall, the university also lost some land. I therefore decided to request the government for more land. On enquiry from the tahasildar (Mr Sambit Nayak), I came to know that there was a patch of 20.5 acres of land on the western side of the campus which was close to the passage given to the villagers to take their plough and bullocks to the agricultural land. These small plots of land of the villagers were not many and along with them, there were plots of government land. The total extent of private lands was four acres whereas the government land was of 16.5 acres. I requested the government to allot these plots of government land and allow the university to acquire the private land in accordance with their procedure and principle. I was very happy that this was approved and the university paid a sum of Rs.3,21,000/- by depositing it with the District Collector. I do not know what happened thereafter. Had the procedure been completed by the university, it would have added about 20.5 acres to its area and the rationale for providing passage route for the plough and bullocks would have lost its strength. The university should treat it as an urgent business and take steps.

Publication of a Monograph of Fakir Mohan

In the conference of Vice-Chancellors of Eastern Indian universities organized by the UGC in Jadavpur University, Porf. Thorat asked me the meaning of Fakir Mohan. He said that Fakir seemed to be a Muslim name and Mohan meant Lord Krishna. What was the meaning of this name and who was this person the university has been named after? I explained to him the background in which this name was given to him by his grandmother besides explaining to him Fakir Mohan's love for secularism. I also told him that Fakir Mohan was in favour of inter community friendship and amity. This was well depicted on a pillar with symbols of all religions in Shantibana, in the heart of Balasore. I also gave a brief account of Fakir Mohan's role in protecting and promoting Odia language and his own contributions to Odia literature as also his role in state building. After this, I felt that a book on Fakir Mohan in English should be published by the university. It should give a complete account of Fakir Mohan. I requested Prof. Rajkishroe Mishra, a retired English teacher of reputation for help in the matter. He kept my request and completed the work in time. Professor Trilochan Mishra, my own teacher of English in Ravenshaw College and former Vice-Chancellor of Shri Jagannath Sanskrit University reviewed the manuscript and M/S Vidyapuri, Cuttack published it on eve of my demitting the office. The book *"Vyasakabi Fakir Mohan: The Precursor of a New Era"* was stored in the university for being presented to relevant people at appropriate time. Some copies were also despatched immediately to different persons of eminence.

Fakir Mohan Archives

Fakir Mohan's life was full of activities of various types. He had varied literary endowments, e.g. writing text books, making translations, writing poetry, short stories, novels and other miscellaneous works. They need be preserved for posterity. His periodical writings, reporting, special essays, book reviews, highly reflective discourses, travel accounts, letters and speeches would continue to charm the present generation. In this context, I had a strong feeling that an Archive should be opened in the university to contain details about Fakir Mohan so that it would be a meeting place for all those who seek to know Odisha of the past, its language, literature, society, people, their culture etc. With this end in view, I got a life size statute of Fakir Mohan built by an artist (Nityananda Sahu) and opened an Archive in the New Campus on 8 March, 2008. Eminent Scholars who have worked on Fakir Mohan (Like Prof. G.N. Dash, Prof. Debendra Nath Dash, Prof. Rajkishroe Mishra, Dr Arabinda Giri, Mr Laxmikanta Tripathy) and few other who have devoted time to discuss Fakir Mohan (such as poet Brajanath Rath, Chandra Kumar Mohanty etc.) were invited to the installation ceremony. Dr Ajit Kumar Tripathy had consented to be the Chief Guest on this Occasion but he could not make it owing to unforeseen work pressure. The Archives was opened and materials collected till then were kept there. The eminent guests advised on how to collect materials. Some of the invitees also offered to donate important documents on Fakir Mohan. I do not know whether the Archive is in existence and has developed as a richer wealth of the university.

Chancellors of the University I worked Under

I had the privilege of working directly under three Governors who were ex-officio Chancellors of the state universities of Odisha. These three were from three different walks of life, one was a retired Chief Secretary, a bureaucrat, emphasizing on rules and procedures, the second one was an eminent Chartered Accountant, a former Minister in the Cabinets of Indira Gandhi and Rajiv Gandhi and the third one was an Advocate of the Supreme court of India. Sri M. M. Rajendran, the retired chief secretary of Tamil Nadu was very aggressive in his behaviour. Rameshwar Thakur, with his pleasant look was very courteous, and at the same time, firm and humane in his approach. He took keen interest in the functioning of the university.

Ever since I was Director, College Development Council of Sambalpur University, I had information about Sri Rajendra's toughness. I had the information about how he took very active interest in university matters. I also realized his toughness in the dialogue which he had with me before appointing me as Vice-chancellor of F.M. University. As far as I know, most of the Vice-Chancellors did not feel comfortable before him since he could easily locate deficiencies in management of concerned universities. I was no exception. He became friendly to me after about one year of my functioning as Vice-Chancellor.

Except for a brief period of about 2 months, all along I was in one university or another of Odisha and, as such, I had first-hand information about the problems that the university administration faced from time to time. I, therefore, was very careful on these points and the progress in these aspects were reflected in every Monthly Report submitted to the chancellor. The Chancellor's Secretariat consolidated reports of all the universities. Every month, in at least 25% of the points of the consolidated Report, F.M. university was praised and other universities were advised to emulate FM university. This trend continued till I demitted the office. I don't know what happened then. I leant from Prof. Adhikari, who became vice Chancellor of F M University in 2014 that the tradition of obtaining monthly work-report on university was discontinued.

About five years back, in course of a discussion in the Raj Bhawan on higher education in Odisha, as a member of a committee constituted by the Chancellor, I made a reference to the monthly report from the universities to the Chancellor. The chancellor, Sri. J. C. Jamir enquired about it. Thereafter, a letter from the Raj Bhawan asked the universities to send monthly reports to the Chancellor.

Shri M. M. Rajendra, like Shri Rameshwar Thakur took very active interest in development of the universities, their teaching programmes, examination schedules, peaceful campus, timely distribution of degrees and diplomas as also holding of Annual Convocations. Each year he had at least, one meeting with the Vice-Chancellors, Secretaries relevant from the point of view of university education and about half a dozen of Ministers (Those of High Education, Finance, Home etc). Solution to most of these problems could be found out by this August body. During Shri Thakur's time, efforts were made by the Raj Bhawan in taking up problems of the Universities on one special occasion, the Chairman, U.G.C. (Prof Sukhadeo Thorat) had a meeting with all the three Vice-Chancellors of Odisha in the Odisha Raj Bhawan in presence of the Chancellor Shri Thakur. The Universities raised some issues which, in their opinion, the UGC failed to appreciate. Prof. Thorat, thereafter, sent a senior Joint Secretary to Odisha and discussed this problem and the ways these could be sorted out. Many problems were sorted out then and there. My university had the approval of the UGC on several proposals.

In course of my stay in the F M university for about five years, I could organize three Convocations. For the second convocation, as per my request, the Chancellor (Shri Thakur) helped the university in having Dr.A.P.J. Abdul Kalam as the Chief Guest in the convocation. Not only did he arrange the Chief Guest, he played a very proactive role in preparing the ill-equipped campus for the President's Visit. I felt immensely grateful to him particularly since the date of convocation was fixed on the day my father expired and the Convocation was held on my father's tenth day (Dashah) of death.

The third convocation held during my leadership of the university had Prof. Rajsekharan Pillai, Vice Chancellor, Indira Gandhi National Open University. In this convocation, since the Chancellor's son had a very serious accident of Delhi, he could not be available for the Purpose. He authorized me to preside over the Convocation. I had to do it. The third convocation was held in the New Campus, at Nuapadhi. By this time, Shri Rameshwar Thakur had been transferred and appointed as Governor of the state to Karnatak. Shri Muralidhar Chandrakant Bhandari occupied his place. Whereas, Shri Thakur had laid the foundation, Shri Bhandari inaugurated the new campus, after one year and six months on the day of the convocation. Prof. Sukhadeo Thorat, Chairman of the University Grants Commission graced the convocation as the Chief Guest. It was a matter of great satisfaction for me that all the three who visited the new campus were full of appreciation and admiration.

Shri Rajendran's kind help in facilitating release of government Order on creation of teaching posts for the university was a great favour to the university. It was on the eve of the declaration of General Election (2004). Had the order not been released on that date, filling up of the posts to prepare for the UGC Visiting committee would have been delayed by about six months. My relation with all the Chancellors was very good and functional.

Retirement from Fakir Mohan University

My second term of Vice-Chancellorship ended on 16th March, 2008 on completion of my age of 65 years as per the university Act. I would have continued for another one year and six months had not the university Act limited the age of retirement to 65 years. However, I had no regrets because I felt that I had made good use of my days in office and had earned a huge stock of love, appreciation and good will from all segments of the local population. Here after, I had no interest to serve any more in any other capacity. A friend and well wisher at Balasore met me before my last day there and requested me to be associated with an institution which he built at Balasore. This institution imparted teaching in Engineering and Management and this friend wanted me to be officially associated with it at a salary equivalent to what I got as the Vice-Chancellor. I wanted to be at Bhubaneswar and even then this friend suggested that I could be in the institute for two to three days in a week, I declined the offer.

Had the institute been located at Bhubaneswar, I would have accepted his offer even without any financial benefit. I wanted to remain active and, at the same time, remain at Bhubaneswar. However, I had the desire to resume teaching which was stopped during my Balasore days. Such an offer also came from a friend (Prof. Verghese, Retired Vice-Chancellor of a law university who worked as professor in Christ University at Bangalore). He wanted me to accept a post retirement assignment at a high salary in a university at Bangalore. I requested Prof. Verghese to excuse me for my inability.

Balasore and me, after retirement

The concluding few months of my tenure in F.M. university were full of activities. I had many things to do for the university within that short period. These were also the days when I did lots of introspection and tried to assess my role as the chief of that institution. Many things were left unfinished or half finished. My apprehension was that my successors might not accord that priority to these or they might have an attitude opposed to mine and, in that case, good things and traditions (as per my perception) might suffer. But I had to satisfy myself that just as I did my best, my successors would do their best, and their 'best' might be better than my 'best'. I should not feel that I am the most intelligent man having a great vision.

When I joined the F.M. university, I had many apprehensions, I might not be befitting for the job. A few friends from Balasore and Bhadrak telephoned me and cautioned me that days at Balasore would be difficult- the people there being very shrewd and complicated. The local people are not dependable, said some of them. I told them that I would be good to every one and work with honesty and dedication. I had also the experience of working with highly unscrupulous colleagues in an earlier place of my work. In fact, they indirectly though, gave me training as to how one should work in an adverse situation. I told my friends that I had the confidence that my Gurudev would lead me in right direction. Before I left for Balasore to join, my father had a piece of advice. A few years before I joined, a Vice-Chancellor of a particular university of Odisha was removed from his position for alleged acts of financial impropriety. Reading from the news papers, he asked me to see all such papers on financial transaction properly before putting signature. I promised to do it. However, I did not have much of that kind of problem. The Registrar of the university was also in charge of Comptroller of Finance in Change. He being a thoroughly honest person, I did not really have any occasion to be worried. The Controller of Examinations was very competent and dependable.

As regards the people of Balasore, I had a totally different experience. They were cordial and highly cooperative. They made me a part of their socio-cultural life. Whenever I asked for some favour to the university, they never said 'no'. It was for their cooperative attitude that I could manage many things of the university in those days of financial crunch. I was delighted to see that, unlike many of their counterparts in other universities of Odisha, the members of the Syndicate did not utilize their positions for financial profit. One member (Dr Harish Chandra Jena), the Chancellor's nominee in the Syndicate never traveled in university vehicles. He came in his own vehicle and never claimed a pie for his tour or duty. In some other Universities, as I saw earlier, some members travelled by bus but claimed TA in hired taxi. This was not the case in Balasore. Some citizens offered their help in developing the garden in front of the office building at Vyas Vihar. Some offered 150 Coconut plants for plantation in the Vyas Vihar campus and make it beautiful. The free support of a contractor facilitated making the Vyas Vihar campus plain, free from bushes of thorns and reptiles. Many such acts of goodness come to my mind. I had built a network of friendship at Sambalpur during my stay there for more than quarter of a century and some of them still have their love and good will for me even after my retirement in 2008. My stay at Balasore was hardly for five years but my circle of friend and well wishers at Balasore is quite big. Almost every week, I get a telephone call from one or the other enquiring about my health and other things, I am thankful to them for this.

A Vigilance enquiry against me

One year after my retirement, some one who had some grievances against me sent letters to all possible authorities indicating therein that I had indulged in corruption during my tenure as the Vice-Chancellor. The matter was enquired by the Vigilance Department of the state government. I heard that some files of the university were taken and pages were Xeroxed by Vigilance people and clerks were frequently questioned. I did not take it seriously because I had not done anything wrong deliberately. It was about six months thereafter that one Inspector of Vigilance telephoned me and asked me to come to Balasore for giving clarification on some points in a vigilance enquiry relating to the university. I requested him to come over to Bhubaneswar since it was not possible for me to go to Balasore. He suggested a date and I accepted it. He did not come for about a year thereafter though I reminded him several times because I wanted to be mentally free form any tension. He, however, had enquired from several people of Balasore and Bhadrak districts and, as he told me after the discussion, everyone had words of love, appreciation and respect for the work I did for FM University. Ultimately, he came to me in 2011 (if I remember rightly). As was understood, the allegations were as under:

(i) I committed corruption in giving university land to private individuals on quid pro quo basis and earned rich profits.
(ii) I renewed the contract of a Book Seller for supply of books without inviting fresh tender.

(iii) I engaged the MES for construction work at a higher rate and thereby made money.
(iv) I was man of bad morals and had such history in all places where I worked.

With regard to allegation (i), I gave details of the crisis relating to occupation of land and also showed copies of letters concerning land, written by me to the Chancellor. He also was surprised to know that a particular patch of land on the southern side and close to the road which was alleged to have been illegally given to a private individual was actually private land, not government land given to the university.

As regards allegation (ii), I showed him copy of a circular from Government of India (Ministry of Finance) forwarded by the then Additional Chief Secretary (R.P.Padhi) to the Colleges and universities. This circular said that the universities and colleges need not invite tender for purchase of books and Journals, I also gave him copy of report of the Good Offices Committee saying that books and journals were not store materials and there need not be any tender to purchase them. A letter from the UGC saying that the colleges and universities need not invite tender for purchase of books was also given to him. university could collect a discount of 10% to 15% on the printed price. I had also copies of the circulars issued by Chairmen, Post Graduate Councils of Utkal and Berhampur universities asking the Heads of Departments to collect 10% to 15% discount on printed Price. I told the inspector that no university invited tender for this except Sambalpur University. Sambalpur started inviting tender in 1990s when Mr. Rajendra Kishore Panda was the Administrator of the university for a short while. The university collected 20% instead of 10% discount after inviting tender. The FM university collected 10%

discount on the printed price till I joined but after I joined, we got 20% discount from a book seller who sold books to Sambalpur University. When the university received UGC grant for books, (Rs.22 lakhs) we invited tender and a local book seller quoted 30% discount and we allowed him to supply books in about seven months. At the end of the 3rd months, we found that he could not supply of books worth Rs.90,000.00. The syndicate cancelled the order re-invited tenders. As a result, two book sellers (Books Corner, Burla and Mishra Book Suppliers, Bhubaneswar) were short listed for this purchase. We allowed them to supply books with 26.5% discount as per books published in India and 20.5 % for those published outside India.

Next academic year, admissions to the newly created Departments of Applied Physics and Ballistics and Social Sciences were done and as the classes started, students and teachers needed relevant books. The time of one year allowed to the books sellers was over. Purchasing books after inviting tender would have meant waiting for at least three to months. I did not take the risk of waiting that long and therefore renewed the contract of the existing suppliers. This, according to the petitioner was my crime.

I made it clear to the Vigilance Inspector that there was no necessity of inviting tender as per the rules. Besides, when the university invited tender the year after my retirement, the percentage of discount on printed price available to the university was only 20%. He collected the copies of the relevant circulars and letters from me.

As regards the allegation (iii), I explained to the inspector that the university entrusted construction work to a central government agency. As per their rates, payments were made. The quality of work of the MES was definitely high. The projects were completed in time and there has been no need to raise the cost of construction. The last point related to my personal character. This could be enquired into by his visiting my previous places of doing work at Berhampur university and Sambalpur University. Also, details about my nature and character could be collected from people of Balasore and Bhadrak districts. Thereafter I have not heard anything about the case and I don't know the status of the case either.

My appointment as a Member of the General Council of NAAC

The UGC organized a conference of Vice-Chancellors of Eastern India in Jadavpur University on 15-16 Sept, 2007. In course of discussion, the chairman of UGC laid emphasis on some new traditions and institutions which should be built by the universities. Among these were choosing time and dates of examination and publication of results, teacher's evaluation by students in post graduate education, organizing employment mela in the campus etc. He was very happy to know that Fakir Mohan University was the only university which had already put all these into practice. He was so much pleased that he promised me, during the lunchon, that he would help me to open a satellite campus of the university at Bhadrak if I submitted a proposal for that. Next month (Oct, 07), he nominated me as a Member of the General Council of the National Assessment and Accreditation Council for three years. This was for the first time that the FM University came to be associated with an important all India body engaged in quality promotion in higher education.

Academic activities after retirement

On return from London, I devoted some time to each of the research scholars whose doctoral thesis could not be completed so far. Four of them (PK Dash, Nihar Kumar Panda, Utpal Devnath and Dibakar Swain) completed their work and were awarded the Ph.D degree. A senior bureaucrat (A.C. Padhiary) who worked for D. Litt. degree has, in the mean time, been awarded the degree. I delivered talks in the different programmes (Seminars, Refresher Courses, Orientation courses etc.) organized by the Utkal, Sambalpur and Fakir Mohan universities and also in many colleges of Utkal, Sambalpur, Fakir Mohan and North Orissa Universities.

The UGC appointed me as Chairman/ Member of different committees for the XI Plan and, in that capacity, I visited several Universities to assess their achievements and needs. That gave me a lot of information on how some of our Universities could adopt special measures to strengthen the university society relationship. In fact, I discussed some of this with the then Secretary, and the Minister, Higher Education Department.

I was appointed a member of a Standing Committee on Exemption by the University Grants Commission (2009-11). All except one in this committee were Vice-Chancellors (in office or retired) and, interestingly, all the members were from all major communities though they were educationists and educational administrators. I loved working in this committee. We were asked to settle problems of thousands of college teachers of Maharashtra as per the directive of the Bombay High Court. This related to career, regularization and promotion of college teachers in states in general and those of Maharashtra in particular. The committee was so aptly constituted that we had no difficulty in providing a solution to the problem.

The Vidya Sagar University (West Bengal) utilized my service in preparation of some of their colleges for UGC assessment. I visited some of these colleges. As Chairman of the "On the Spot Enquiry Committee" appointed by the UGC, I Visited ten colleges affiliated to Burdwan University. This committee was asked to physically examine the proper or otherwise utilization of UGC grants of rupees one crore to each of the colleges for construction of Women's Hostels. Some of these colleges made proper use of the UGC money and constructed Hostels for Women students but a few others committed irregularities which the committee reported to the UGC.

During this period, we came across a very embarrassing situation while conducting enquiries in one of these colleges. The UGC grant was for construction of a two storeyed building. The college had exhausted the entire amount without completing even the ground floor. The principal could not properly explain the situation before the committee. In the presence of the committee, the Head Clerk of the college, who was asked by the Principal to bring a particular file, came and vomited poison like things against the Principal. He openly criticized the manner in which the principal handled the matters relating to construction of the Hostel. No amount of threat by the principal could silence him. This situation spoke a lot on the state of affairs in the college. While the committee was coming back from the construction site, a team of teachers met us and requested us to have interaction with the Teachers' Association which remained waiting in a hall nearby. The committee had already smelt the situation in the college when the Head Clerk exhibited an unusual behaviour before it. The Principal also had tried to prejudice the committee against the teachers who, he said, were highly political and faction ridden, some supporting the CPM and others supporting the newly elected Trinamool Congress government. The committee, therefore, chose not to meet the teachers. In fact, the committee was to examine whether the funds provided by the UGC were spent in accordance with rules and procedures. These could be objectively found out from the documents and interaction with the principal, and the construction committee as also the Engineers associated with the work. This was also as per UGC Norms.

An unforgettable experience

One thing which I cannot forget about was in relation to my visit, as a Member of the XI Plan committee of the UGC, to a private university at Chitrakoot. It is situated at a distance of about 120 km from Allahabad. Very close to it flows the river Mandakini. Chitrakoot, as such, is famous as a place of pilgrimage because Lord Ram is said to have remained there with Sita and Laxman for some time during his days of *vanvash*. One finds various Ashrams named after great *rishis* (said to have established them) on the way to Chitrakoot from Allahabad. I found hundreds of people standing in queue under the scorching rays of the sun to have a darshan of the deities in the Ashrams. In fact, I felt like getting down from the car and visit the sacred place but then, I thought, it would be improper for me to do so because I had come for some official business. Chitrakoot is a very beautiful place and the sacred memory attached to it makes a visit to it a privilege for a Hindu. The university is unique in many ways. It is a private university established for the physically disabled by a saint who is completely blind. On our arrival in the university, the Vice-Chancellor informed all of us that the Chancellor (the said saint) would like to meet the Members of the XI Plan UGC Team before they visited the Departments and utilities of the university. we agreed. The Vice-Chancellor introduced us one after another to the Chancellor. Then came the surprise. To each one of us, he asked in English the state from which he came but the rest of interaction was in the local language of the team member. When I said that I came from Odisha, he talked to me in Odia and spoke on Lord Jagannath, he sang loudly the Bhajan composed by Salabega (*Ahe Nila Saila Prabal Mato Baran*........). This was a famous Odia Bhajan. Then he said, a physically disadvantaged person gets immense solace when he has a darshan of Lord Jagannath who looks like a physically disabled one, possessing immeasurable abilities despite His apparent lack of ears, leg etc. So also, the physically disadvantaged is otherwise enabled and what is necessary for us is to discover his latent faculties, equip him properly and develop him into his best, both for him and for the society. All of us were really mesmerized by his words, his way of speaking, his knowledge of so many languages (Odia, Tamil, Punjabi, Urdu, Hindi and English) and his approach to life.

Our surprise did not end here. When we visited the Departments, we found that all students were physically handicapped in one way or the other. Many proved that their physical disadvantage did not stand on their way to development. The blind could walk comfortably, he could write on the Black Board, the one who had no hand or leg did not find it a problem in day-to-day life. We were glad to know that the students were from most of the states of India, particularly from the North and North East India though there were a few from Andhra Pradesh and Gujarat. In the evening, there was a cultural programme organized by the university but the participants were the physically handicapped students. The legless could dance and the handless could fight. The committee was highly impressed with the university, its students, its teaching programmes and other enabling schemes. It did what it could as per the guidelines of the UGC in recommending grants under the XI Plan period.

On the last day of the programme when the work was over we visited Sati Anusuya Ashram, Ram Tirth and all the places important from the point of view of Ramayan we felt privileged to have touched the sacred soil. I personally cannot forget this trip.

Court Cases against me

I received summons from the Judicial Magistrate of Bhubaneswar and Balasore in connection with two defamation and compensation petitions submitted by one Dr. BK Naik and his wife Kasturi Naik. The former was a Professor in F M University and the university had removed him from service during my period of Vice-Chancellorship. Subsequently, he had appealed to the High Court which asked the university to reconsider his case. My successor reconsidered the case and reinstated him with the condition that he would not claim salary for the period when he was not in service. After retiring from the university in May, 2009, he filed a case in the court of Balasore SDJM claiming compensation for Rs.5 lakhs from me. He alleged that I was responsible for his loss of job and the loss of job defamed him. His wife also, alleged that her prestige and position in the society were affected because of the removal of her husband from service. The cost of her prestige, she calculated, was Rs.50 lakhs. Thus, together, I seemed to earn a liability of Rs.55lakhs.

Whereas Dr. B.K.Naik filed his defamation case from the court of Judicial Magistrate, Balasore, his wife Kasturi Naik filed it in the office of the Judicial Magistrate, Bhubaneswar. This made their objective obvious- they wanted to take revenge against me since they felt that Dr. Naik lost his job for me. When I met the then Hon'ble Chancellor Sri Muralidhar Chandrakant Bhandare and showed him the petition, his immediate reaction was, "He wants to harass you in running from one place to another". He advised me to appeal to the High Court to kindly allow trial of both the cases in one court only. I obeyed his advice and the High Court as per my prayer allowed both the cases to be tried in the court of the Judicial Magistrate, Balasore. The Hon'ble Chancellor also directed the university to meet the expenses to be incurred in the cases. The case from Bhubaneswar was transferred to Balasore in about six months. Thereafter, neither Dr. Naik, nor his wife nor their authorized Advocate took any interest in the case. No body attended the court.

Friends who helped me at Balasore
Rabindra Mohan Das: While felicitating me on my appointment as the Vice Chancellor, F,M.University, my Vani Vihar days' friend Rabi (Rabi Narayan Das, IAS) advised me to be in touch with his father in law Rabindra Mohan Das (popularly called Rabi Babu) in case I had any problem at Balasore. I knew of Rabi Babu as a leader of honesty and dedication and had the opportunity to interact with him on coalitional politics in Odisha during my period of doctoral research. As such, I would have met him in view of his contribution to the cause of establishment of Fakir Mohan University. And my friend's advice strengthened my decision to meet him. I joined the university on 17th March, 2003at 12 Noon and met rabi Babu at about 5 PM. At his residence. Thereafter, I visited the *Khir Chora Gopinath* temple to seek the blessings of the Lord in the evening.

As I felt, Rabi Babu was very pleased to see me and

he advised me to seek help in case I had any problem. Rabi Babu was always ready to help the needy. He had quite a good number of permanent guests at his residence. In fact, at a particular time, he alone from his family lived in that crowded house. Very simple in his lifestyle and habits, he was an idealist. He was a highly lovable and respected person.

Discussing matters with Rabindra Mohan Das

It was because of him that large number of people from Balasore and Bhadrak came together, formed the Balasore Educational Foundation and fought for a university at Balasore. Rabi Babu was the Secretary and the Treasurer of the Educational Foundation. He was assisted by people of all political parties. Significant among the leading public figures of the area who supported Rabi Babu were Maheswar Bag (former Congress minister), Dr. Bijaya Giri, Dr. Harish Chandra Jena, Dr. Radha Devi, Baidyanath Sarangi (retired ADM), Advocate Chandra Kumar Mohanty, Bhuban Das, Sukumar Nayak, Sarat Chandra Das and poet Brajanath

Rath etc. Despite the deadlock resulting after the creation of North Odisha University, the Fakir Mohan University could be a reality because of the image and standing of Rabi Babu in Odisha political circle. The Education Minister Sri Bhagabat Prasad Mohanty had great respect for Rabi Babu and because of this, he made all possible efforts for creation of the university at Balasore when Giridhari Gomango became the chief minister in July, 1999.

If anybody reasonably should claim a lion's share in the credit for establishment of F M University, it was probably Rabi Babu. At an advanced ag, he sat under the umbrella to supervise the construction work of the three storeyed building at Vyasa Vihar under the scorching rays of the Sun and also under the heavy shower of rain. There is no comparison to the physical and mental exertion he had to undergo. He lovingly called me workaholic Vice Chancellor. The university could get the land, building and the library which Rabi Babu had built from the college established to facilitate creation of a university.

As a mark of respect for him, the F M University awarded the first D.Litt (Honoris Causa) to Rabi Babu in 2005. During the Vice Chancellorship of Prof. S P Adhikari, a statue of Rabi Babu was installed in the small garden in front of the three storeyed building at Vyasa Vihar. I was present there on that day and the building in front of which it was installed was built under Rabi babu's care.

Dr. Harish Chandra Jena: In course of my stay at Balasore, I came in close contact with a person. He was Dr Harish Chandra Jena, a very successful surgeon who had his own clinic at Balasore. He earned a lot and spent lavishly though he had no bad habits. He was liberal towards poor patients. Besides treating them free, he also donated medicine to them.

I came to know him as the nominee of the Chancellar in the syndicate of the university. Somehow, I had a bias against non-academic people who sought positions in the syndicate. Some of them actually did not know anything about the business of a university. Some, as I had seen elsewhere, were locals who did not have any fruitful engagement and, as a result, they milked the university for their sustenance. Even some academicians were mad for syndicate positions to inflate their ego. I apprehended that this doctor could be one such person. I was totally wrong. This gentleman was a rare person. He spent a lot of money in financing the University Foundation Movement and in treating guests visiting Balasore in connection with the university. He never interfered in the university administration during my vice-chancellorship. He never took a pie from the university when he undertook journey to attend university business.

When the faculty selection process started, Dr Jena came to me and said something which helped me to understand him well, He said, "Vice-Chancellor Sir, I am a local man, I motivated people to join the university foundation movement and took different types of assistance from them for the movement. It is natural that when the university is going to make appointments, they come and approach me to help them as a member of the syndicate. In case, I telephone to you, please treat it without any importance. You choose the best among the candidates". This spoke eloquently on him and his commitment to the university.

The height, of his happiness was visible on two occasions – the day the government sanctioned the teaching posts for the five Departments and the day on which teaching started in the newly opened five Departments.

He carried loads of sweets and other eatables on these occasions and distributed among the students, teachers and the employees. A special ladoo of about half a kg was gifted to me but I did not eat it owning to its heavy sugar content. He invited all VIPs coming to the university for dinner at his place. He loved entertaining people without any expectation.

If the one acre of land close to the original old campus of F.M. University could be acquired by the university, it was, possible owing to the sincere help of Dr. Jena. I had a feeling that the one acre retained by the Balasore Education Foundation for itself while donating six areas to the newly founded university on 11 July, 1999 was lying useless. Its future, I thought, was also so. It should also have been given to the university for fruitful use. When, in course of a discussion, I expressed my feeling, Dr Jena, then President of the Balasore Education Foundation, opened his heart to me. He said that I should make efforts for acquiring this land. He apprehended that after him and Rabindra Mohan Das, the Education Foundation could run into wrong hands and the land could cause problem both for the Foundation and for the university. He said, since most members of the Foundation loved me and trusted me, I should make an appeal to them for this. This appeal would not go in vain, Since Dr. Jena had several health problems at this stage, he apprehended that end to his life could come anytime. He advised me to be prompt and I appealed to the Foundation in a letter. Dr. Jena brought it before the Governing Body of the Foundation and got its approval accorded. However, since the foundation had a loan of 3,60,000/- the Foundation asked the university to help in paying the said amount to the Foundation and enable it to pay back the loan. I got it approved by the syndicate and got the cheque for 3,60,000/- sent to the Foundation. The university added the precious land and the two storeyed bulding standing on it to its assets. This was hardly a month before Dr. Jena's demise. I remember him so much because he devoted his time, resources and mind for the university at Balasore. He was a rare person and a very good friend.

Dr. Choudhury Satyabrata Nanda: During my days at Balasore, I came in contact with another person who could be meaningfully associated with developments in the university. He was Dr. Choudhury Satyabrata Nanda, an eminent doctor who, after serving as a government doctor for more than 25 years, chose to become a permanent resident of Balasore though he belonged to Jiginpatpur village of Salepur (Kendrapara district). His reasons for such a decision were many, the most important of these was the literary culture of Balasore and the important role played by the illustrious sons of Balasore in nation and state building. As a doctor, he has earned a very good name, he is more known as a humanist, a person committed to help the needy. He is philanthropist and derives pleasure in financing some students in their education including expensive medical education.

Dr. Nanda is a prolific writer, he has already proved that the literary culture of Balasore has been conducive to his development as a literary person. As far as I have seen his works, his focus has almost always been on the youth, the younger school and college going boys and girls. "The youth should have a rational mind, he should be guided by matter of facts, he must be scientific in his attitude and, at the same time, he must have respect for his own society and the country" – He said so. That is why, while explaining scientific principles, he pushed the ethical and moral values into their minds.

Dr. Nanda extended many types of help to the university when the latter needed it much. The newly established university had no provision for health care of the employees and the students. As per my request, he opened a Health-care-Centre in the university building. A room was allotted for this purpose where he kept all the instruments used in examining patient.

He brought, along with him, all materials needed for the purpose of treatment. He also brought the sample medicines for distribution in this cell. He came for 2 hours (3 PM to 5 PM) and provided medical help to the employees and students. Besides doing all these free, he permitted all from the university to come to his clinic at his residence and avail of free help. He got particular books translated and got them printed (at his cost) in the name of the university, thus added to the university's fame and finance.

He donated the prescribed amount of money to the university for creation of a Gold Medal for the First Class First in MA (Population Studies). He also has been, I am told, very active in aiding the university in many other ways such as creation of a number of Annual Prizes for academic excellence, games and sports and also organization of Alumni Association. It may be pertinent to say that Dr. Nanda, despite his busy schedule in the clinic carved out some time for reading and writing. I am also told that he had his D.Sc. Degree for his research carried on for several years. He is probably the first D.Sc. of the F.M. University. Both Dr. Nanda his wife are highly hospitable and I availed it once years after I left Balasore.

Niladri Vihar to Durga Madhav Nagar: Shift of Place of Stay

We had planned to spend our post retirement days comfortably. Instead of always staying at Niladri Vihar, we would spend time with our children since in our plan of things, we have treated them equally without any discrimination. However, we would make Niladri Vihar our headquarters since the house at Niladri Vihar is one of our achievements in life. It has given us a permanent address. We are some of the early inhabitants of this area and we know most of its dwellers. They also know us and have, quite clearly, expressed their love for us. This place has grown into one of the best residential areas of the Bhubaneswar Municipal Corporation. My daughter Arati stayed at Jayadev Vihar with her family and she could frequently visit us. My sister-in-law (Anu) Stays at Gajapati Nagar. She and her sons (Srikant and Susmeet) called on us quite frequently and took a lot of our care. We, therefore, decided to stay at Niladri Vihar as long as we are able to manage ourselves. We would shift to one of our childrens when we fail to manage ourselves or one of us leaves the other permanently. But providence had a different direction.

Following Suman's untimely passing away in August 2009, Renu had several health problems. She already had diabetes and now she had orthopedic problem. She found it difficult to cook food but did it because there was no alternative. I had also serious health problems and I had to be hospitalized many times. Yet, we did not think of leaving Niladri Vihar.

We, then, tried to find out a part time cook and a domestic maid servant. A part time cook, staying in the Niladri Vihar slum area was available. Within a week, a tribal girl from Kandhamal also was available for domestic work. We thought things would be all right thereafter. In fact, problems started then. The cook stayed with her family and the domestic maid servant stayed with us. She slept in the ground floor and we slept in the first floor, one day, within about a week of joining of the domestic maid servant, there was a burglary in the house. One window of our bed room in the ground floor was broken open. We had kept most of our valuables and costly clothes in the Godrej Almirah kept in that bed room. Along with this these, certificates of children (including the three Gold Medals which my daughter Arati received from the university for her excellence in graduate and post graduate examinations) were there. The burglars laid the standing Almirah on ground and took away everything valuable from it. The said maid servant was in the adjacent room and, as she said, she heard sounds of the window being broken open, Almirah being laid on the ground and sound of opening the Almirah. She chose to come to us in the upstairs only after the burglars left. She could have come earlier to inform us. The room in which the miscreants were active was under lock and key from outside into the dining space. The said maid servant could have easily and safely come to us to give information. Why she did not do so was a question. The police could have examined that.

    Hearing from the maid servant about it, I came down stairs and found that everything was alright except the burglary in the said room. I went to Chandrasekharpur Police Station to lodge an FIR about the burglary. Then came the dog squad and thereafter the Inspector of Police (Deepak Mishra) came and visited the site. Hearing from the Police Station, some journalists came, took photographs of the broken windows and the floor of the said bed room.

    When Inspector Deepak Mishra came, I told him

that I suspected foul role of the maid servant and the part time cook. The maid servant, ever since she joined, talked to people over phone for long hours and at night. Besides, both the new recruits were seen silently talking to each other. On the day preceding the might, both of them talked to a person and took him to the back side of the house. The cook had an adult unemployed son.

I gave all details and points of suspicion to Mr. Mishra who instead of subjecting the maid servant and the cook to investigation, advised me to immediately ask the tribal girl to leave because, he felt, she was a minor tribal girl. I told him that she was 18 years old but without caring for it, he advised me to dispose her off immediately. He promised to recover the lost goods in about a week but it is already more than 3 years.

Loss of property worth about Rs. 20 lakhs was a shock no doubt. Loss of Gold Medals and the Certificates of my children gave me greater shock. Worst of all was the behaviour of the Police officer. After this incident, I felt that staying away from children at this stage of life may not be good. Thus came the mental preparedness in both of us to stay with one of the children. Arati and Biswamohan gave that chance. When the construction of their new house was over, they visited us and, in course of discussion, they said that we should stay near them. Accordingly, we chose to stay in the ground floor of their new house independently. My son-in-law along with his parents, stayed in the first floor. Since Feb, 2019, we are at Durgamadhav Nagar.

It was a very judicious decision for us. Had we not come to stay near them, our life during the Corona pandemic would have been miserable. We thank God for His kindness.

■ ■

Black Eagle Books

www.blackeaglebooks.org
info@blackeaglebooks.org

Black Eagle Books, an independent publisher, was founded as a nonprofit organization in April, 2019. It is our mission to connect and engage the Indian diaspora and the world at large with the best of works of world literature published on a collaborative platform, with special emphasis on foregrounding Contemporary Classics and New Writing.

www.ingramcontent.com/pod-product-compliance
Lightning Source LLC
Chambersburg PA
CBHW020523080526
44583CB00013B/717